Version 1.0 - February 2020

Copyright © 2020 Dale Young
All rights reserved.
ISBN: 9781654591335

Praise for *The Identity Key*

We know God better when we know ourselves better. Dale has spent decades discovering who God has designed him to be and he has provided the rest of us with a handy guide for discovering more about ourselves. I highly recommend this book to anyone who wants to accelerate their own self-awareness. It's a journey worth taking!

~~ **Diane Dotson**, Founder, One80 Life

I believe that Dale has a true heart of connection and a desire to help others know who they are so that they can continue on their journey to significance. By reading this book I think you will feel that connection and gain some tools to help you discover who you are.

~~ **Dave Barnes**, Mission Director, Frisco Bible Church

Coach Dale is a difference-maker. He knows that who we are is more important than what we do. That is why we are called human beings, not human doings. This book does a great job of telling his story and allowing you to see the steps to take to learn the answer to the question, "who are you". When you know the answer to that question you can then become a difference-maker in your own way.

~~ **Sam Morrison**, Head Ninja, Your Admin Ninja

Dale put his finger on the pulse of our desire for authentic, genuine leaders. Our identity is key to unlocking our significance, as his title states. But Dale goes beyond an explanation to share his experience with the tools, and the traps, of a pursuit of significance. He challenges us to search not only ourselves, but also our Creator and his word to understand our identity and how it fits our created purpose. Only you can do the work, but as any great coach would do, Dale guides and encourages. This exercise will make a difference in your life and legacy if you pursue it.

~~ **Mike Henry**, Founder, Follower Of One

*This book is dedicated to
the people and staff of
Frisco Bible Church
and especially
Pastor Wayne Braudrick
for modeling relational community,
providing a fertile area for growth,
and supporting me with love in some
of my darkest moments.*

Thank you!

Acknowledgements

No book is created alone. Many people have poured into me over the years, through training, coaching, mentoring, and friendship. All of these people have contributed in some way to the thoughts, ideas, and experience of this book. **Thank you** to all of you!

In the "Who Am I?" chapter, I have a timeline of some of the important locations (tools) on my journey. If you were part of the people who helped me while I was in one of those seasons, I would like to extend a special **thanks** to you in addition. And if for some reason we are no longer in regular communication, this would be an excellent time for you to reach out to me so that I can thank you properly!

To the people and staff of Frisco Bible Church, thank you for all you've done for me over the years. (See the Dedication at the front of the book.)

A special **thank you** to the people who reviewed this book in all of the drafts, and helped make it better:
- Sam Morrison
- Diane Dotson
- Dave Barnes
- Mike Henry

For the actual creation of this book, my **thanks** go to Sam Morrison and her team of Ninjas at Your Admin Ninja.[1]

---

[1] youradminninja.com/

CONTENTS

Foreword 1
Links and References 3
Chapter One: Introduction 4
Section One: Identity Connections 12
    Chapter Two: Who Am I? 13
    Chapter Three: Who Are You? 16
    Chapter Four: Connections 19
        One80 Life 20
        The Three Legged Stool 21
        Smooth Stones 23
        Relationship Bullseye 24
        EQ vs IQ 28
        RARE Leadership 31
Section Two: Assessments 32
    Chapter Five: General Assessment Comments 33
    Chapter Six: Four-Quadrant Personality Assessments 36
        Four Temperaments 38
        DISC Assessments 39
        Everything DiSC 40
        Colors 42
        Personality Plus 43
        Smalley's Animals 44
    Chapter Seven: 16-Type Assessments 45
        MBTI 46
        Keirsey Temperament Sorter 47
    Chapter Eight: Enneagram 48

Chapter Nine: EQ Assessments 50
Chapter Ten: StrengthsFinder 51
    WeAlign Strength Alignment Process 55
Chapter Eleven: Spiritual Gifts 56
Chapter Twelve: Combo 58
    COREmap 59
    RightPath 60
    SHAPE 61
Chapter Thirteen: Other Assessments 62
Section Three: Identity Tools 64
    Chapter Fourteen: Writing / Journaling / Diaries 65
    Chapter Fifteen: Affirmations 67
    Chapter Sixteen: Music 69
    Chapter Seventeen: Books 70
    Chapter Eighteen: Podcasts 72
    Chapter Nineteen: Experiential-Based Retreats 74
        Pathways 75
        The Road Adventure 77
        Walk to Emmaus, Tres Dias 80
    Chapter Twenty: Coaching 81
    Chapter Twenty-One: Spiritual Growth 85
    Chapter Twenty-Two: Groups 89
Section Four: Recommendations 91
    Evaluation 94
    Final Thoughts 95

Foreward

One of the keys to unlocking your significance, purpose, and calling in life is to understand at a deep level who you were created to BE. There are many workshops, tools, assessments, coaches, and retreats which will give you pieces. And yet there is always another, deeper layer to yourself. Ultimately you have to integrate all the pieces into your own awareness and be able to succinctly answer the question: "Who are you?"

Why would you read this book?

My hope and prayer is that you get some of these things out of this book:
- Encouragement — to start or continue your own identity journey;
- A deeper understanding of the major factors that play into your identity;
- A fresh perspective on yourself and your relationships;
- An overview of some of the pieces that contribute to your identity;
- A perspective from someone who has traveled the road before you and can maybe save you some time by pointing you in a better direction, or keeping you from a trap;
- And a few ideas or concepts that may be new to you.

Why did I write this book?

My overall **why** is:

> Shining Christ's light on people's unique potential, so that they will embrace their possibilities and grow in their significance.

There are many other books on success, significance, and identity out in the world… why add another?

Frankly, there are not many **new** ideas here. However, to use a cooking analogy, there are not many new ingredients in the world. But chefs come up with new recipes all the time. How do they do it? They combine different ingredients in different ways and with different spices, to come up with their own "signature dish" or "special sauce."

As with any "why?" question, there are always multiple reasons.
- I've done a lot of work around my own identity.
- I've helped a lot of others with their identity work, as a:
  - volunteer in organizations;
  - leader;
  - mentor/friend;
  - and as a coach.
- Perhaps my "special sauce" will have impact on some.
- As you can see in my **why**, it's part of my significance to help other people with their significance.

Therefore, it is my calling to add my voice, my uniqueness, my "special sauce" to the mix.

Links and References

There is a multitude of links in this document. There are two reasons for this:
- I don't want to increase the size of this book with material that you can find easily on the web; and
- You can dig deeper on the areas where you are most interested.

The links will show up as footnotes in the printed version. Note that I'm not going to include the "http://" in front of the link, in order to shorten it and make it more readable.

In the Kindle / eBook format the links are clickable links.

Links and other references are notoriously hard to type in correctly, and they tend to go stale easily. Therefore, I've created a page[2] on my website. This has all the links in live, clickable electronic form.
This page will be updated with the latest information and links.

---

[2] coachdale.com/lsk_identity/

Chapter One: Introduction

*"Life is a journey.
Your dream is the compass.
Passion is the fuel."
~~ Dale Young, 2011*

The Identity Key

Grand title, isn't it? What did you think you would get when you saw that title? Did you think I would tell you the key to your identity?

If so, I'm sorry to disappoint you.

Your identity is not something someone else can tell you. It's something you have to discover for yourself. Something you have to dig for, to mine for, to work for.
- Is it work? **Yes**.
- Is it valuable? **Very**!
- Is it worthwhile? In the end, it's one of the **most worthwhile** things you can do with your life, because it is part of unlocking your significance, your purpose and your calling in the world.

This book is not a scholarly treatise. It is a compendium of my most valuable experiences in the growth of my identity — and ultimately of my own search for significance. You will get a broad overview of a lot of things, with some deep dives into certain areas where I've spent a lot of my time, all of it with a perspective on how this might be useful to you. If you get one nugget of truth, or you save one hour of your time by zeroing in on what you want to pursue, or you save one hour of your time by avoiding what will NOT work for you, then the book has been of value. My hope is that there will be several of these for you!

The Identity Question - Who Are You?

The basic questions for ANY information gathering or problem solving are called the "Five Ws."[3] They are: Who, What, When, Where, Why ... and many people add How.

The identity question focuses on the Who question, and in particular **"Who are you?"**

Like most deep and meaningful questions, this is not a question that can be answered lightly or without a lot of self-work. We'll cover just how deep this can go in a future chapter, and indeed, through the rest of the book.

For now, suffice it to say that the "Who are you?" question focuses more on your **being** and less on your **doing**. However, who you are today has been greatly influenced by your past, by how and when you grew up, what kind of parents or other authority figures you had in your life, and what you've accomplished to this point in your life.

Consider a Bonsai Tree.[4] These trees are shaped and restricted by the Bonsai artist, but underneath is a full tree. One of the keys to answering the "Who are you?" question involves, as much as possible, separating these "nurture" influences from your "nature" — not to deny the nurture, but to understand where you could be with different influences. And to give you the choice, if you want and it makes sense, to choose different influences going forward.

The Journey to Significance

We all go through stages in life, and you can be in different stages in different areas of your life at the same time.

I've seen multiple models of different areas:
- Family, Personal, Business, Physical, Mental, Spiritual, Financial, Service (my Wheel of Life[5]).
- Personal, Professional, and Spiritual (Pathways)
- Financial, Physical, Relational, and Spiritual (Team National)

---

[3] wikipedia.org/wiki/Five_Ws
[4] wikipedia.org/wiki/Bonsai
[5] coachdale.com/wheel/

- The Life Balance Wheel from *Becoming a Professional Life Coach*[6] (8 areas)
- The Basic Life Account from *Living Forward*[7] (9 areas)
- The "Align Your Life"[8] Inventory from PCCI[9] (16 areas)

These models are not better or worse depending on how many areas they have; it all depends on whether a model works for you or not. I would recommend you try several, or use the one your coach recommends, as almost all professional coaches are familiar with this idea.

No matter how you slice it, almost all of these areas ask you to measure yourself on a scale from worst to best. Typically, they use a 1 for worst and an 10 for best.

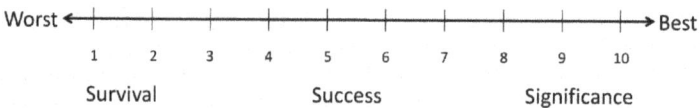

Today however, instead of the areas, I'd like to concentrate on the stages — the scale. Let's put some words to that scale:
- 1 - Survival
- 5 - Success
- 10 - Significance

Survival — when you are in Survival mode, you are just getting by, and you often feel like you're not even doing that. For instance, if you look at this in the Financial area, it's easy to see when you're in Survival — there's more **month** than there is **money**, or there's no regular income at all, or you don't have enough money to pay your bills.

Success — when you are in Success mode, things feel like they are working and you're doing okay. Maybe not great, but okay. In the Financial area, there's more money than month, you're paying your bills, you have enough for the necessities and maybe even some

---

[6] smile.amazon.com/Becoming-Professional-Life-Coach-Institute/dp/0393708365/
[7] smile.amazon.com/Living-Forward-Proven-Plan-Drifting-ebook/dp/B012H10GBW
[8] professionalchristiancoaching.com/inventory
[9] professionalchristiancoaching.com/

luxuries. Note that most of the time, Success is focused on you and your immediate family.

Significance — when you are in Significance mode, you're having an impact on the world. You are not only taking care of you, but you are actively helping a larger community to grow and achieve both Success and Significance.

Note that you can be in different stages along different areas. For example, you could be in success in the Financial area, in Survival in the Physical area, and in Significance in the Spiritual area — all at the same time.

Many people get confused because they assume that to go from Success to Significance is doing more of the same that got you from Survival to Success. This is especially true in the Financial area. If you can afford all the luxuries you want, does that equate to Significance? The world is full of books and testimonials of people who will resoundingly say **"NO!"** Check out Bob Buford's book *Halftime: Moving from Success to Significance*[10] as one of the classics in this area.

Finding YOUR Significance, what will cause you to feel like you've made a difference, is the major topic of the Lifesong Keys series. This particular key, *The Identity Key*, is just one of three keys to unlocking your significance.

About Lifesong

Music[11] is a big part of my journey. I've always appreciated music. Music puts me in touch with my emotions, my sense of feeling and wonder. Since the mid 2000's I've been creating playlists of music, and since 2011 I've been creating annual playlists of my favorite Christian songs from the year.

---

[10] smile.amazon.com/Halftime-Changing-Your-Success-Significance-ebook/dp/B000SG9IUE/
[11] see: Chapter Sixteen: Music, page 67

In the late 2000's, I was fascinated by — and I am still enamored of — the song *Lifesong*[12] by Casting Crowns.[13] The entire lyrics are meaningful, but the chorus especially so:

> Let my lifesong sing to you
> Let my lifesong sing to you
> I want to sign your name
> To the end of this day
> Lord led my heart was true
> Let my lifesong sing to you

I've probably listened to *Lifesong* thousands of times in the decade-plus since I first heard it. When I first got into life coaching, I actually set up my company as Life Song Christian Coaching. It's part of my goal, my mission, to make sure to honor God with my *Lifesong*.

Lifesong to me is a metaphor for the journey to significance.
Let's restate that: **YOUR** journey to significance.

About Unlocking Your Significance

If Lifesong is the journey to significance, then having keys to unlock any roadblocks on that journey are important. These "Unlocking" books are mental maps for your journey.

My goal with these books is to give you a sense of the landscape, not describe every point of reference in detail.

For example, I live in the Dallas area of Texas. I want to make a journey from where I live to my brother's house, who lives in Amarillo. To get from my place to his, having a map — whether a physical sheet of paper on which the map is printed, or a software (GPS) version, or even a mental model (because I've made that journey many times) — is necessary to help me navigate from here to there. However, the map does not dictate that as the only journey. If I want to go a restaurant in Fort Worth, I can find that on the map as well. The map just provides details about what is, it doesn't evaluate whether one is better than the other, and it doesn't specify your starting or ending points.

---

[12] wikipedia.org/wiki/Lifesong_(song)
[13] wikipedia.org/wiki/Casting_Crowns

In a similar way, these *Lifesong Keys: Unlocking Your Significance* books are maps, but instead of geographic locations, they are maps to tools I have used or developed to help you on your journey to significance. Of course, there are others, but these are the ones I have tested and found useful.

To use an analogy, there are locations on this Unlocking atlas/map which are unknown, at least to me the mapmaker. As old maps used to say, "here be dragons.[14]" That's not to say that those locations are bad or unknown to everyone, you have experienced tools that I haven't.

Note however, that these books are NOT guides. A guide says start at Point A, takes you along a pre-planned, pre-defined journey, and it ends at Point B. Guides can be useful, but they don't know enough about you and your circumstances to know what would work best for you. In the physical world, a tour guide most often takes a group of people along a pre-planned itinerary. For extra cost, you can hire a personal tour guide who knows the area where you plan to travel, and can enhance your experience, but each trip is customized for the person. In the journey to significance, the personal tour guide equivalent would be a life coach.

While this is not a guide, there are some general recommendations in the final section. Once you have an idea of the kinds of things that can help you along your identity journey, this can help you put them in some kind of "smallest and easiest" to "largest and hardest" order, with some self-evaluation questions for you to choose a potential starting point. However, since each person is unique, take these recommendations and apply your own wisdom to them.

So think of these Unlocking books as "maps" — or whatever similar metaphor works for you. They will point out:
- some interesting things that you haven't heard of before but might be useful on your journey;
- things you might have been exposed to but didn't quite understand; and
- things you are already familiar with, but didn't know how they fit on your journey.

Just call me the Journey Coach and MapMaker.

---

[14] wikipedia.org/wiki/Here_be_dragons

About this book

This particular book, *The Identity Key*, is about one key of the significance puzzle.

Knowing your identity allows you to answer the question "Who are you?"

Section One contains my story and some of the important elements to help you understand this particular map of tools, experiences, assessments, people, and organizations — or generically, just "tools." In a map, this would be the front matter to help you understand what this collection of locations has in common.

Section Two contains the assessments for helping you in your identity journey. In a map, this would be one major category. You could think of this as the actual roads on the map.

Section Three contains the other tools that I know about for helping you in your identity journey. In a map, this would be "everything else" besides the roadways — for instance, cities, states, lakes, mountains, points of interest, etc.

Section Four is the recommendation section mentioned above. In a map, this would be the back section containing the references.

Are You In Your Sweet Spot?

A sweet spot[15] on a racquet or bat is the area that will give the greatest result. When you connect with the ball in this location, you get the most power and velocity of the ball in the direction you wanted. You can be off from that area even part of an inch, and you won't get the impact or velocity. Sweet spot[16] has become a more generalized term over the years for "an optimum combination of factors or qualities."

---

[15] wikipedia.org/wiki/Sweet_spot_(sports)
[16] lexico.com/definition/sweet_spot

In sports, people don't always hit the ball with the sweet spot. Professionals in sports connect with the sweet spot a lot more often than amateurs.

Similarly, the people that are further along their journey to Significance are connecting with their sweet spot a lot more than others.

Let me encourage you that you can always get better at hitting your Sweet Spot. Even Tiger Woods, who had one of the greatest golf swings ever, has changed his swing[17] five times in his career, to work better with his current physique.

This series on Unlocking Your Significance is designed to give you some examples, stories, and tools to allow you to get to your sweet spot more often.

---

[17] golfdigest.com/story/an-exclusive-look-at-tiger-woods-new-swing

Section One:

IDENTITY CONNECTIONS

Section One contains my story and some of the important elements to help you understand this particular map of tools.

In a map, this would be the front matter to help you understand what this collection of locations has in common.

Chapter Two: Who Am I?

> "The reasonable man adapts himself to the world;
> the unreasonable one persists in trying
> to adapt the world to himself.
> Therefore, all progress depends on
> the unreasonable man."
> ~~ George Bernard Shaw

Before asking "Who Are You", I think it's only fair to give you an idea of "Who I Am." Here is my Life Statement:

> I am a loved and complete child of the One True King, shining Christ's light on people's unique potential, so that they will embrace their possibilities and grow in their significance.

People who have been through experiential-based trainings such as Pathways[18] or The Road Adventure[19] will recognize this as my **contract**. (More about the Chapter Nineteen: Experiential-Based Retreats[20] in Section Three.) It is my "Who is Dale" statement. This statement has changed and morphed over the years as I have grown in my understanding of self. It is the shortest and clearest form of the essence of my identity that I have been able to produce thus far. (Astute readers will also note that it contains my "why" statement.)

This contract is an affirmation that reminds me of who I am, and centers me. I state it to myself every morning.

However, it is the culmination of a lot of history — and many people reading this would like a bit more history, so here is a brief list some of the more important dates and events that helped shaped my identity, so that you know a bit more about me. This will be very high-level because details would be lengthy and boring. You are welcome to skip or skim this section! Some more detailed parts that pertain to my identity journey will be expanded in the rest of the book.

---

[18] pathwayscoretraining.org/
[19] theroadadventure.org/
[20] see: Chapter Nineteen: Experiential-Based Retreats, page 71

- Prior to 2000: I had graduated college, had worked for more than 10 companies in around 20 different roles, and was married with no kids.
- 1998 - Dedicated my life to Jesus. I had previously prayed to accept Jesus, but I had no life change. This was a major shift in priorities. I started to dedicate a large part of my time to growing in the Spiritual area.
- 2000, January - Applied Solutions Inc. (ASI), a startup company. Part-owner, VP, and Manager of Consultants. Started with nothing, did great, named to Entrepreneur Magazine "Hot 100" fastest growing companies in America in 2000 and 2002. Imploded due to personnel disagreements in 2004, shut down to avoid bankruptcy and lawsuits.
- 2004, April-July - Attended Pathways. First contract, lots of emotional growth and healing.
- 2004, October - Consultant at Stonebridge. Still employed there, although since 2016 it has been part-time.
- 2004, November - Started attending Frisco Bible Church. Became a member in 2005.
- 2005-2009 - Volunteered at Pathways
- 2006, October - Attended Walk to Emmaus in Amarillo, TX.
- 2007 - Heard about Life Coaching as a professional career. Investigated, but did not pursue.
- 2008, March - Certified in COREmap. Over the next 4 years I administered over 150 COREmap sessions.
- 2009, summer - Found and read *Christian Coaching* by Gary Collins. This presented a blend of Life Coaching with a Christian foundation.
- 2010, summer - Volunteered at Dallas Emmaus Community Walk to Emmaus. I continue to volunteer there as I can.
- 2011, January - Started coach certification at Professional Christian Coaching Institute (PCCI).
- 2011, July - Signed my first paying coaching client.
- 2013, December - Certified Professional Life Coach (CPLC) certification from PCCI.
- 2015, July - Certified Everything DiSC and Five Behaviors of a Cohesive Team Facilitator.
- 2016, March - Divorced after 32 years, no children.
- 2016, April - Still at Stonebridge, moved to a part-time role of 20 hours per week
- 2016, December - Certified Professional Leadership Coach (CPLC) certification from PCCI.

- 2017, May - Transformational Leadership Coach and On-Demand Facilitator.
- 2018, January - Associate Certified Coach (ACC) from International Coach Federation (ICF).
- 2018, January-February - Attended The Road Adventure.
- 2018, July-present - Started volunteering at The Road Adventure.
- 2019, April - WeAlign Executive Coach

For the purposes of this book, let me elaborate on a few points.

For most of my professional career, I worked in Information Technology (IT). In the early days, I was a Computer Nerd.[21] Mind you, before Nerds were popular. And yes, I was socially awkward, I had limited Emotional Intelligence (EQ), but I had a good heart and a good brain. However, because I can cry easily (like at a sad commercial easily), I had learned to hide my heart. One of my coworkers tagged me as Mr. Spock.[22] I embraced that role and did my best to hide my emotions.

But God was working on me, I was growing into a complete human and not just a one-dimensional person. I moved into management of technical people and had to grow in how to relate to them. I moved into leadership and consulting, more growth. I dedicated my life to Christ and started growing as a Christian.

While the pieces of my identity were growing, my self-perception of them was not keeping up. I still thought of myself — if I thought of myself in those terms at all — as a Technologist, a Nerd. It was through the Pathways training in 2004 that my self-perception started to catch up. I realized I was actually more of a relational, people person. This was cemented in March 2008 during my COREmap certification, and I fully embraced that I was NOT the Spock persona.

Since then, I have been a full participant in my growth journey towards identity and significance. The timeline above testifies to the fact that I have been moving, growing, learning, and making a difference not only in my own life but in the lives of others.

---

[21] dictionary.com/e/dork-dweeb-nerd-geek-oh/
[22] wikipedia.org/wiki/Spock

Chapter Three: Who Are You?

"Who are you?"
~~ Lorien, Babylon 5

Just to show you how much of a nerd I am (or maybe was), and how God can use everything for his glory, let me tell you where I first seriously considered the "Who are you?" question. This may seem like its off-topic, but I want to set the context and the background, because it highlights the challenge of answering the "Who are you?" question.

The cause of my consideration was actually an episode of my all-time favorite TV show, Babylon 5[23], in March 1995, close to the end of the second season. Babylon 5 is a science-fiction show that was revolutionary for its time for several reasons. It is set about 200 years in the future, humans have made contact with alien races, and have gone to the stars. In this universe, humans are not the oldest or most superior, and they are not the most technologically advanced, they are actually somewhat backwards technologically.

There were several things that made Babylon 5 ground-breaking. For one thing, it was conceived as a five-year story arc, a novel for TV. This was totally new in the science-fiction genre and was fairly new anywhere on TV at that time. It ran for five seasons from 1994 to 1999, 22 episodes per season, with five additional made-for-TV movies. Very unusual for the time, the special effects were all computer generated with no actual models, and it was done on microcomputers instead of larger, more expensive computers. Another thing that was revolutionary was the quality and the consistency of the writing. J. Michael Straczynski (JMS) created and produced the show and wrote 92 of the 110 seasonal episodes (84%) — including every episode in seasons 3 and 4, a feat never before accomplished in American TV.

JMS had a background as a journalist and was very familiar with the five W's of journalism. Part of this influenced his concept for the show. The entire five-year story arc centered around a conflict of massive proportions of two ancient races who had deep theological differences. Each race had one of the W questions as part of their philosophy. One race focused on the "Who are you?" question.

---

[23] wikipedia.org/wiki/Babylon_5

Getting back to the particular episode that made me consider the "Who are you?" question. The title of the episode was "Comes the Inquisitor", and it focused around one of the heroines of the story having to answer the "Who are you?" question. Essentially, the heroine is taken — actually, tortured — through multiple levels (at least six) of answering the "Who are you?" question. This particular paragraph from the script is the Inquisitor commenting on the heroine's difficulty of answering that question:

> "What a sad thing you are, unable to answer even such a simple question without falling back on references and genealogies and what other people call you. Have you nothing of your own? Nothing to stand on that is not provided, defined, delineated, stamped, sanctioned, numbered and approved by others? How can you be expected to fight for someone else when you haven't the fairest idea **who you are**?"
>
> (This reference is from *Babylon 5, The Scripts of J. Michael Straczynski, Volume 4*, page 23 of the "Comes The Inquisitor" script.)

In the end, the heroine answers the question based on her faith, her belief in her destiny, and her willingness to die in her cause. That satisfies the Inquisitor.

JMS himself comments in his notes about this episode:

> "More than the voices of anger or opposition or criticism, for an artist of any sort the most lethal voice is the quiet voice of reason that makes us forget who we are and what we can do, that lulls us to sleep and keeps us safe, since to follow our dreams as we intend can lead only to disappointment.
>
> However well intentioned, that voice is the enemy and always will be."
>
> ~~(*Ibid*, page 56 of the "Riding The Elephant" section.)

And although I did not realize it at the time, this episode planted in me a desire to really understand who I was. And in some regard, it was a monumental time in my life, because a few years later I dedicated my life to Christ. With the benefit of hindsight, this question was one of the keys that brought me to Christ.

Because I realized that for me, I needed a foundation to believe in, a foundation that was unchanging, and a foundation that was based on love and kindness. I found all of this in the person of Jesus Christ.

Chapter Four: Connections

> Then God said, "Let us make man in our
> image, according to our likeness."
> ~~ Genesis 1:26a

As humans, we were created to be in connection with others, and in community with other like-minded individuals. The biblical story of creation is God wanting new connections, not with robots who only do His will, but with people made in his image.

The One80 Life

My good friend Diane Dotson expresses this connection theme beautifully in her work, the **One80 Life**.
She says that we are created to be in:
- Connection with God;
- Healthy connection with others;
- And connection with True Self.

Diane uses the idea of a "lens" with her One80 Life Model. When you have an issue, and you examine that issue through the One80 Life Lens, you consciously look at the issue in regard to the three bullet points above.

I have found myself amazed at how issues that are so blurry when I first consider them become very clear when examined through this lens.

As an example, I had come up with an idea of a fund-raiser to help a group of people. I had recorded a video and used the name of an organization in the video. The leader of the organization found out about it and requested that I remove the video because he thought it could be interpreted as a solicitation for the organization. I was very discouraged, even depressed, over this request — but Diane walked me through the One80 Life Lens, and I saw where I had failed to consider the ramifications. I saw where I would have been breaking connection with all three (God, other, self). After that, I was happy to comply with the request to remove the video.

You can find out more about Diane's model at her web site.[24]

Thought question: which of your connections (God, others, self) needs the most improvement?

---

[24] one80life.com

The Three-Legged Stool

One model that is simple to communicate that seems to illuminate this for many people is to envision a three-legged stool. This stool is strong and stable when each of the three legs is strong and stable. The three legs are:
- Relationship with God;
- Healthy relationship with others;
- Relationship with true self.

These individual legs are strong when the relationships are strong, and love flows in that relationship.

I did not understand this for many, many years. I suffered from a lack of relationships and connection growing up. Like the bonsai tree, I was shaped by my nurture and unhealthy connections in all three areas, even though my nature was seeking for those connections.

One of the keys to healthy relationships, is growth in emotional intelligence, or EQ. In many ways, my identity growth has been tightly coupled with my growth in EQ.

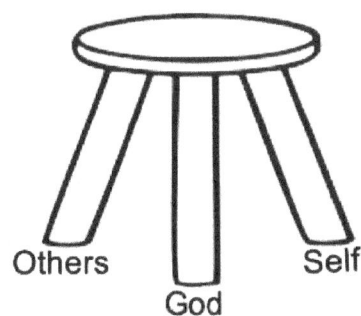

Thought question: when you consider your relationships, which ones need improvement?

Smooth Stones

> Instead, he took his staff in his hand and chose five **smooth** stones from the wadi and put them in the pouch, in his shepherd's bag. Then, with his sling in his hand, he approached the Philistine.
> ~~ 1 Samuel 17:40, CSB

In August 2019, I was able to be with my friend Chuck Couch in Santa Fe, New Mexico. Chuck took me up on a mountain and showed me some sites, one of which was different groves of aspen trees. Chuck pointed out that all the aspen trees within the grove were lean, very tall and very straight. And yet the root system did not go down very deep. Where they grow on the mountain, the soil is not that deep, because you quickly hit solid rock.

The question arises, how can trees be so tall with such shallow root systems? The answer is that all the root systems are interconnected. As a matter of fact, what looks to us like individual trees, is just part of one large massive organism. There is one root system connecting all these trees. So in one sense, the whole grove of trees is really just one organism, one plant.

Like the grove of aspen trees, humans are interconnected as well. Perhaps we don't have a visible root system connecting us, but we do have interconnections.

Pro-Bible or pro-evolution, it's a historical fact that until the 19th century humans existed and lived mostly in small villages. These tribes were typically less than a 500 people. In a tribe of this size, everyone was known, and everybody had a place. There was accountability to each other, and for each other.

I believe that one of the major reasons for the chaos in today's society (mass shootings, lack of civility, the tendency to shout and whine instead of discuss rationally) is that we've "grown out of this." For example, in almost every mass shooting in the last 30 years, it has later came out that someone (a parent, a friend, a coworker, whoever) will say something like: "yeah, that guy was going through ..." or "that guy changed (or shifted) a few weeks ago." In the communities of the past, someone would have stepped up and taken action that would have prevented the bad outcome. We don't have the accountability that was inherent in smaller societies. We've lost our sense of connection and community.

My church, Frisco Bible Church, focuses on an annual theme. In September 2019, the theme for the next 12 months was announced as "smooth stones." Everyone knows about the story of David and Goliath. The quote above is part of that story. Inspired by the question in the above passage, "Why did David pick up **smooth** stones?" What was special about the smoothness?

What's special is that smooth stones will fly a lot faster, straighter, and truer than rough stones. David had a much greater chance of hitting his target with smooth stones.

So the next question arises. How do stones become smooth? Through the rubbing and tumbling motion, the friction with other stones, typically in water. Rocks "knock off rough edges" with collisions with other rocks. As people, we "knock off our rough edges" through interactions with other people. Often, these interactions are unpleasant when they are happening, but they help us grow. When looked at through the One80 Life[25] Lens, we see that they are helping us connect with God, with our true self, and develop healthy connections with others.

Most of the assessments in Section 2 and the tools in Section 3 help us to "smooth off the rough edges."

Thought question: what rough edges need to be smoothed off from you?

---

[25] see: One80 Life, page 19

Relationship Bullseye

While we are all interconnected, some connections are closer and more important than others. As with the aspen trees, the closer they are (physically), the more intertwined their root systems, and the bigger effect one will have on the other. In a similar way, people who are closer to you relationally have a more significant impact on you.

It is worthwhile to spend some time and understand where your relationships fit in your life. We all know that you don't want to be sharing detailed personal information with everyone on the internet, or your identity will soon be stolen and you will be bankrupt! However, someone in your life does need to know these details.

Between those two extremes, there is a gradient that occurs. You can think of this in terms of a bullseye. The red circle in the middle is the group that is closest relationally, and the area outside the bullseye is the furthest. Let's look at some typical categories.

- **Core** - This group is the closest. You know each other's details and secrets. You talk multiple times per week, if not multiple times per day. This group could be close family or really close friends. They are people that you're gone through a very difficult time with and you've helped each other survive. "The closest friendships are developed in the foxhole."
- **Close Friends** - Not quite as close as the Core, you still likely talk once a week.
- **Extended Friends** - People you talk to once per month, or maybe you go for long periods of time without talking but when you do get back together, it's like you haven't been apart.
- **Tribe** - You're part of the same organization(s), you believe the same things, but you've never spent the time to get close. Likely you know them well enough that if a sudden shift in behavior occurs, you'll notice and maybe even get someone involved.
- **Crowd** - People you know, kind of, and you interact, but not often.
- **Followers (Fans)** - They know who you are, possibly because of your position or role, but you're not close and you don't necessarily know much about them.

While these are typical categories, everyone will be unique in how many and how they define the "rings" of the bullseye. However, as you get closer to the Core, the number of people in each circle goes down. For instance,

- **Followers (Fans)** - Could be in the millions for some people. Is likely in the thousands in today's social media world.
- **Crowd** - Small thousands.
- **Tribe** - Maybe as many as 500 or 1,000, but likely less.
- **Extended Friends** - Maybe 70, likely less than 100.
- **Close Friends** - Around a dozen.
- **Core** - Three to six.

You just don't have enough time in the week to be touching base with more Core and Close friends.

Here's what I use for my numbers, although they do vary a bit (nothing is ideal in this world):

- **Core** - 3
- **Close** - 12
- **Extended** - 70
- **Tribe** - 500
- **Followers** - more

I base these numbers on the life of Jesus. Everybody recognizes the 12 as the number of Apostles that he chose. He had an inner Core group of Peter, James, and John - the 3. What about the 70? In Luke 10, "the Lord chose 70 others" (some translations say 72). Then there was the tribe of 500 that followed him around. And there were the crowds of followers where he feed the 5,000 and the 4,000.

When you adopt this way of organizing your relationships, you get clarity that helps you make decisions around how to spend your time. Your time is your most valuable resource, because you can never make more time. When you spend too much time with the tribe, your closer friends suffer because you don't have the time for them.

You may find that some people are in the wrong area on your target. Some may be too close to the center and you need to move them out. Some may be too far out and you need to move them in. If you have a toxic friend who is in your close relationships, and you need to move them out, you can do it gently in stages - instead of talking to them every week, move it to every other week and then once a month. Once they are firmly in another circle, you can decide whether to move them out even further.

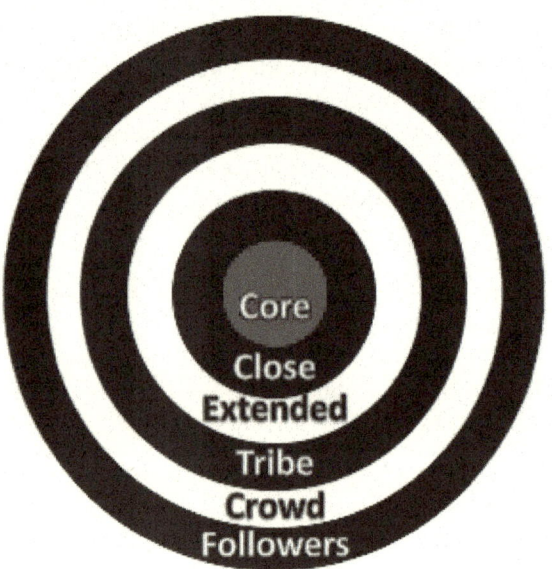

Thought question: which relationship do you immediately know needs to be changed to a different circle?

EQ vs. IQ

Working in IT for so many years, I've seen so many people who, for whatever reason, close themselves off from other people. They don't relate well; they don't open up and share. This is partly due to the fact that the industry seems to attract loners and individuals. That's probably one of the reasons why I was a good fit in the early days, since it did not require me to work closely with a team. The phenomenon is not unique to the IT industry. I have seen it in other industries as well.

In some sense, it's a positive feedback loop – you focus on growing your individual (often technical) skills at the expense of relationships, you get rewarded for doing a good job, and you continue the cycle. It often comes to a crisis point years later. It could be any of these:
- A family relationship caused by aging (or dying) parents;
- A promotion into an area of higher responsibility at work;
- An issue with children and their choices;
- A divorce or other separation;
- The loss of your job, and you can't find a new one because your skills are no longer in demand;
- Even a mid-life crisis, where you realize you're not where you expected to be.

Building Relationships

Your identity is intertwined with your relationships. No matter what your role in developing yourself as a leader, relationships will impact everything you do. If you are bad at developing relationships, that will work against you. If you are good at developing and fostering relationships, that will work for you. Let's explore several aspects of building relationships.

EQ defined

Emotional Quotient (EQ)[26], Emotional Intelligence (EI), Emotional Leadership (EL), and Emotional Intelligence Quotient (EIQ) are referring to the same thing; at least for all of us that don't specialize in

---

[26] wikipedia.org/wiki/Emotional_intelligence

those fields. It is the capability of individuals to recognize their own emotions and those of others, discern between different feelings and label them appropriately, use emotional information to guide thinking and behavior, and manage and/or adjust emotions to adapt to environments or achieve one's goal(s).

The model introduced by Daniel Goleman[27] focuses on EI as a wide array of competencies and skills that drive leadership performance. Goleman popularized the term Emotional Intelligence in his 1995 book of the same name. Goleman outlines five main EI constructs:
- Self-awareness – the ability to know one's emotions, strengths, weaknesses, drives, values and goals and recognize their impact on others while using gut feelings to guide decisions.
- Self-regulation – involves controlling or redirecting one's disruptive emotions and impulses and adapting to changing circumstances.
- Social skill – managing relationships to move people in the desired direction.
- Empathy – considering other people's feelings especially when making decisions.
- Motivation – being driven to achieve for the sake of achievement.

Goleman includes a set of emotional competencies within each construct of EQ. Emotional competencies are not innate talents, but rather learned capabilities that must be worked on and can be developed to achieve outstanding performance. Goleman posits that individuals are born with a general emotional intelligence that determines their potential for learning emotional competencies.

You can increase your EQ via any number of tools. Literally hundreds if not thousands of assessments, trainings, books, companies, seminars, programs, and websites are out on the market. Some of these have a very direct impact on EQ, some more indirect. Most professional coaches have experience with improving EQ and often can direct you to other resources as needed.

Thought question: which of your five EI constructs would give you the greatest return if you spent time improving that one?

---

[27] wikipedia.org/wiki/Daniel_Goleman

RARE Leadership

In 2019 the book that had the most impact on me was *RARE Leadership*[28] by Dr. Marcus Warner and Dr. Jim Wilder. This book has impacted my view of leadership, relationships, brain science, accountability, habits, identity, and connections. I highly recommend reading and studying this book! Below are some of the many nuggets of gold in the book:

Brain Science helps explain EQ:

> … recent developments in brain science now reveal that leadership skills are learned in a different way and in a different area of the brain than management skills and academic studies. We now know how leaders can train this powerful brain system to produce full engagement in their team and develop a high level of emotional intelligence that keeps them plugged into a renewable, high-octane source of motivation. (*RARE Leadership*, p. 19)

What this tells us is that people who naturally developed high levels of EQ made better leaders, and that anyone can learn how to train the brain to have better EQ.

The difference between leadership and management:

> Many leaders, business people, pastors, team leaders and influencers never receive any training in leadership. This contributes to mistaking management for leadership. Management is the efficient accomplishment of tasks. Leadership is producing and maintaining full engagement from our group in what matters. The RARE leaders we wish to emulate inspire us because they do this well. Now, we will show you how it is done. (*RARE Leadership*, p. 20)

Left Brain (slow-track):

> There are two systems in the brain that are often oversimplified as "left brain" and "right brain." The one that is dominant on the left is the **slow-track system**. By using conscious thought, the slow-track system operates more slowly, but it is, of course,

---

[28] smile.amazon.com/Rare-Leadership-Uncommon-Increasing-Engagement/dp/0802414540

> what we notice consciously. The slow track is optimized for management. Its primary job is to monitor results and provide explanations and solutions to the problems we face. The slow track gets most of the attention in leadership development. (*RARE Leadership*, p. 26)

What has been called "leadership development" in the past is technically "management development"! And that's one of the reasons that the leadership development movement has overall has had such erratic (i.e. poor, unrepeatable) results over the last 20 years.

Right Brain (fast-track):

> But did you know that there is a system in the brain that operates faster than conscious thought? We call it the **fast-track** or "master" system. People have known for years that there are things happening in the brain we cannot quite catch consciously. While most people have been looking below consciousness for that activity, we are only now discovering there is activity above consciousness. This supra-conscious action does its work faster than we can "keep up" consciously. Its primary job is relational reality. *Who am I in my world?* must be clear before I can think about other things. The fast-track system controls how we regulate our emotions, how we remember who we are, who our people are, and how it is like us to act (that is, acting like the self God gave us). In other words, it is our identity center. (*RARE Leadership*, p. 26-27)

The Right Brain / Fast-Track system runs faster than consciousness, so it seems to "just happen" to us! And it is focused on, of all things, identity!

Brain Speed and Habits:

> Both the fast track and slow track in the brain can develop habits. To be a good leader you require a diversity of good habits in both fast (leadership) and slow (management) systems. Habits live in the white matter of the brain, and what gives them their power is that white matter runs up to 200 times faster than gray matter. ... The conscious thought that we have been calling the "slow track" actually operates fairly fast, updating itself with a new state five times every second. Identity processes we have been calling the "fast track" operate even faster, updating six times every second. But this is all gray matter speed. Gray matter is very flexible and can figure out

> new reality and paths as it goes. However, to keep from getting bogged down, the brain creates "habits" that are prepackaged responses to known situations. Habits take a month or more to grow because the brain has to wrap the habit nerves in white insulation, and that takes some time. Once the habit is properly insulated, that cluster will run up to 200 times faster than gray matter. Habits are the fastest. (*RARE Leadership*, p. 29)

Habits are super fast! That's why you have to develop habits for both fast and slow tracks, so that you can keep up. But notice — habits take a month or more to grow! It's not just about how many times you perform the habit, but it's also about creating the white matter in the brain that will give it the speed.

Identity and Connection:

> Choice runs in the "slow track" of our brain. What, then, runs in the fast track that has executive control? The answer is identity. Who we are determines what we will do and identity operates faster and more powerfully than choices. Identity's power over choice does not fit our rational mindset. In addition, our brain thinks of who we are not only as an individual but as a group identity as well. Group and individual identities are not the same, but they also cannot be separated. I always understand myself in reference to others like me. (*RARE Leadership*, p. 46)

Your identity is both individual AND group! That is why connections are so important, and why the One80 Life[29] Lens is such a powerful tool.

Thought question: what was the most surprising part of these excerpts of RARE Leadership for you?

---

[29] see: One80 Life, page 19

Section Two:

ASSESSMENTS

This section contains the assessment tools that I know about for helping you in your identity journey.

In an atlas, this might be one type of item on the map, for instance, all the roads.

Each type of assessment has its own chapter so that it will be easy to locate in the table of contents.

Chapter Five: General Assessment Comments

> I made my own assessment of my life, and
> I began to live it. That was freedom.
> ~~ Fernando Flores

To provide some structure to this section, I will start each Chapter with a series of "Why? / How? / What?" questions:
- The "Why?" question attempts to give you some ideas of why that particular chapter might be valuable to you.
- The "How?" question details the theory behind the assessment(s).
- The "What?" question goes into more details about the actual test and the results.

General Comments about Assessments

All assessments *can be* useful in answering the identity question of "who are you?", but you do have to be careful to apply the results from the assessment through the One80 Life[30] Lens model. For every assessment, ask these questions:
- What is God revealing to me?
- What are my feelings about this? Is this really my true self?
- What do the other people in my Core and Close circles (from the Relationship Bullseye[31]) agree or disagree about this?

Another factor to consider when evaluating an assessment is how much time, money, and effort was applied to get the result. For example, there are hundreds of Facebook quizzes that will show you funny things, theoretically based on your Facebook profile, but often these are just randomly generated. Those are not worth a lot of consideration. But if you invest significant time or money on an assessment, you should seriously consider the results, even if you immediately disagree with the result. It just might be that it is showing you something about yourself where you have a blind spot.

---

[30] see: One80 Life, page 19
[31] see: Relationship Bullseye, page 23

There are other factors to consider as well. Assessments may not be accurate or precise[32], due to many factors:
- Social factors, e.g., people have one personality at work and a different one when out with friends.
- Respondent faking, because of a perceived "right" answer.
- People believing the assessment is more valid than it really is, because they like the answers.
- Respondent confusion, i.e., nature vs. nurture.

A few personal words about this "nature vs. nurture" idea. As you know, I was a nerd. And yet I had the privilege of taking dozens of personality assessments over the years. I used to think it was because companies were trying to figure out the strange IT personality, but looking back, it might have been that they were trying to figure out **me**, since I wasn't the "typical" IT nerd. You see, I always liked talking to the people who actually used the programs or systems that I was working on.

I remember eventually starting to track my results on these dozens of assessments. Most of them were a version of a DISC assessment, so it was easy to see that I always tested out as a DC - mostly D (Dominant) with quite a bit of C (Conscientiousness). This was so much so, that I took the COREmap[33] about five times and always came out to their equivalent of DC.

When I was going through the COREmap certification, the instructors were looking at everyone's results, and how they had showed up for the multiple days of the certification process. They saw something in my results which they commented on, and I had a very emotional moment when I realized that my C (Conscientiousness) was *conditioned* by how I was raised (the nurture), and that I naturally had a lot more I (Influence) by nature. This was a case where I was sincerely not aware of who I was naturally, because of years of conditioning as well as working in environments where that was rewarded.

All of that to say: be sure to evaluate any assessments carefully through the One80 Life Lens before integrating them into your answer to the "who are you" question.

---

[32] wikipedia.org/wiki/Accuracy_and_precision
[33] coremap.com

Thought question: which assessments have you taken, and do you agree with the results?

Chapter Six: Four-Quadrant Personality Assessments

> The single biggest problem in communication
> is the *illusion* that it has taken place.
> ~~ George Bernard Shaw

This chapter is called "Four-Quadrant Personality Assessments" because they all attempt to generalize human personalities into four general areas based on two dimensions. These are also called "temperament assessments" based on the Four Temperaments.

Why might you consider a Four-Quadrant Personality Assessment?

Understanding personalities improves your EQ. If you already have a high EQ, a personality assessment won't provide a lot of boost, but if you have a low EQ, this can help. It can also provide a common language for a team to understand each other better and work together with less friction.

How do Four-Quadrant Personality Assessments work?

The idea is that people can be grouped into one of four quadrants. Each person has a dominant way of acting, and a secondary way. By understanding each of the four quadrants and how they interact with people in the other quadrants, you can modify your approach and improve the relationships.

What are the general details?

The concept of the four quadrants is simple. Think of a large plus sign ("+"). The plus sign has a horizontal bar and a vertical bar. Question one is posed with two opposite dimensions and you choose one side or the other of the horizontal line. Then question two is posed, again with two opposite dimensions, and you choose one side or the other of the vertical line. Depending on your answers, you end up in one of the four dimensions.

I have actually used this technique with a live audience and had them move to their respective quadrants in the room. I then ask a series of questions and see how each of the four quadrants answer differently. The questions that I use are:

- Q1. Are you more extroverted or more introverted? (Alternatively, this could be "Are you more fast-paced or moderate-paced?")
- Q2. Are you more of a task person or a people person?

Each four-quadrant assessment essentially does this same thing. The more repeatable assessments don't ask you the questions directly, but they ask a series of questions around each of the two dimensions. The most repeatable assessments will detect if your answers are very consistent around that dimension, and if they are not, they will continue to ask more questions to determine where you fit — adaptive testing[34].

You have likely been exposed to one of these tests at some point. There are literally dozens, if not hundreds, of these — and the most popular of them have dozens of implementations. I will cover a few of the ones I know about below.

---

[34] wikipedia.org/wiki/Computerized_adaptive_testing

Four Temperaments

Let's start way back at the beginning.

The four temperament[35] theory is the great-great-great-grandfather of all personality assessments. It is a proto-psychological theory which suggests that there are four fundamental personality types: sanguine, choleric, melancholic, and phlegmatic. Greek physician Hippocrates[36] (c. 460 – c. 370 BC) described these terms, and associated them with the ancient theory of humorism[37]. Hippocrates developed this into a medical theory. Galen[38] (AD 129 – c. 200) used the terms for the idea of temperaments, or physiological reasons for different behaviors in humans. His two dimensions where hot/cold and dry/wet, taken from the four elements.[39]

Many others over the years expanded this concept. It has been rejected as medical science, but the debate is still out for psychological fields. It is certain that this theory has influenced most personality assessments, including the ones described after this.

---

[35] wikipedia.org/wiki/Four_temperaments
[36] wikipedia.org/wiki/Hippocrates
[37] wikipedia.org/wiki/Humorism
[38] wikipedia.org/wiki/Galen
[39] wikipedia.org/wiki/Classical_element

DISC Assessments

DISC[40] is the most popular personality assessment. It is based on the Four Temperaments[41]. DISC is a behavior assessment tool based on the DISC theory of psychologist William Moulton Marston[42], which centers on four different personality traits:
- D - Dominance (D),
- I - Influence (I),
- S - Steadiness (S), and
- C - Conscientiousness (C).

DISC has hundreds of variations, from free on-line versions to expensive in-person versions. Since the concept is simple and was not copyrighted/trademarked, it is replicated in multiple ways by multiple people. It is often included as a piece in other combination assessments.

Most DISC assessments will use these two questions to determine the quadrants:
- Q1. Are you more extroverted or more introverted?
- Q2. Are you more of a task person or a people person?

However, many tests will modify one or both of these slightly to make their test unique. And they might use slightly different words; I've seen some tests that use Security for the S instead of Steadiness.

A Google search[43] for "disc assessment" returns over 53 million results. Adding the word "free" reduces this to 38 million. Many of the free versions require an email or some other form of sign-up. One of the versions that does not require a sign-up is the Open-Source Psychometrics Project DISC Assessment[44]. If you are interested, you can try several and see which work best for you.

---

[40] wikipedia.org/wiki/DISC_assessment
[41] see: Four Temperaments, page 36
[42] wikipedia.org/wiki/William_Moulton_Marston
[43] google.com/search?q=disc+assessment
[44] openpsychometrics.org/tests/ODAT/

Everything DiSC

(* I am Everything DiSC certified, since 2015.)

The Everything DiSC[45] assessment is owned and administered by John Wiley & Sons. It is delivered mostly by independent organizations and practitioners like myself. It is a one of the best DISC assessments on the market in terms of accuracy and precision[46]. Wiley has put a lot of time, money, and effort into the validation of the product. It is accurate because of the extensive validation of assessment results to real-life behaviors, and it is precise because of the repeatability of the assessment. Wiley uses "DiSC" with a lowercase "i" to distinguish their DiSC product from the generic DISC instrument.

The Everything DiSC plots a "dot" on a circular field of the four DiSC types and each potential combination. The dot location around the circle shows you which type/subtype you are most like, and gives you an idea of how you can stretch to act like other types. The closer to a type your dot is, the easier it will be to act like that type. In addition, the distance of the dot from the center shows how much you are naturally inclined to encompass your type. Here is my Everything DiSC result:

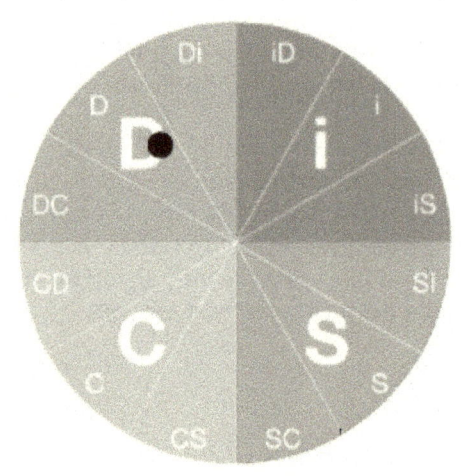

---

[45] everythingdisc.com/Home.aspx
[46] wikipedia.org/wiki/Accuracy_and_precision

Everything DiSC is a computer based assessment, with the results available to the administrator immediately. The administrator can choose to make the results available to the participants immediately or later. The Workplace result is a 20 page document which shows your DiSC type and gives ideas on how to work with other DiSC types.

In addition, Wiley has developed their base DiSC assessment into specialized assessments for Workplace, Management, Sales, and Work of Leaders. The Workplace assessment is the base. The Management, Sales, and Work of Leaders assessments add on specialized information; typically, these reports run 24 to 28 pages.

Wiley also has a multi-source assessment that they brand "363 for Leaders." This type is commonly called 360-degree feedback, and solicits the assessment results not only from the subject individual, but also from people who are in the subject's job and life, typically people "above", "below", and "peer" in the organization. These types of feedback from others can be very enlightening.

The Everything DiSC is very useful in any organization with multiple people, because as the number of people grow, the overall cost per test declines. I have used it with individuals, in organizations as small as four, and in groups as large as 50, but I know of others who have done it with groups of several hundred.

The general feedback on the Everything DiSC and the improved results of organizations can make this assessment valuable and cost-effective to many organizations.

Colors

There are a lot of "color" assessments in the marketplace. Each of these assessments assign a color (typically red, blue, green, and yellow) to one of the quadrants.

Part of my issue with these assessments is that from one to the other, they may assign different colors to the same quadrant. That makes it difficult when you have one assessment that assigns Red to the Dominant quadrant, but you're discussing with a different person who thinks Red is the Influence quadrant. That is why I much prefer using the DISC system.

Here are a couple of the dozens or hundreds of color personality assessments on the market.
- The Hartman[47] Personality Profile - ColorCode[48]
- True Colors[49]

---

[47] wikipedia.org/wiki/Hartman_Personality_Profile
[48] colorcode.com/choose_personality_test/
[49] wikipedia.org/wiki/True_Colors_(personality)

Personality Plus

Personality Plus[50] is the first book in a series of books written by Florence Littauer[51] and based on the system of the same name developed by Cynthia Furlong Reynolds.

The test in the book has two series of 20 questions each. In the first series of strengths, you choose one of four positive words that "most" applies to you, in the second series of weaknesses, you choose one of four negative words that most applies to you. You transfer your choices to the scoring sheet, which has the words in the correct column, then you add up the columns. The result is four numbers, one for each column. The column names (and their corresponding DISC types) are:
- Powerful Choleric   (D - Dominant)
- Popular Sanguine   (I - Influence)
- Perfect Melancholy   (S - Steadiness)
- Peaceful Phlegmatic (C - Conscientiousness)

I first heard of Personality Plus in the early 2000's when John Maxwell[52], best-selling leadership author, mentioned it in one of his trainings.

---

[50] smile.amazon.com/Personality-Plus-Understand-Understanding-Yourself/dp/080075445X
[51] wikipedia.org/wiki/Florence_Littauer
[52] wikipedia.org/wiki/John_C._Maxwell

Smalley's Animals

Gary Smalley[53] took the four temperaments and developed a short (and generally free) assessment but used animal names instead of the dated form of the temperament names. I haven't been able to track down exactly when and where this assessment was first popularized, but it is part of his book *Making Love Last Forever*[54], which was published in 1997.

The animal names (and their corresponding DISC types) are:
- Lion   (D - Dominant)
- Otter   (I - Influence)
- Golden Retriever   (S - Steadiness)
- Beaver   (C - Conscientiousness)

---

[53] wikipedia.org/wiki/Gary_Smalley
[54] smile.amazon.com/Making-Love-Last-Forever-Smalley/dp/0849940869

Chapter Seven: 16-Type Assessments

More isn't always better. Sometimes it's just more.
~~Barbara Benedek

This Chapter includes two assessments that extend the four-quadrant model into 16 types.

Why might you consider a 16-type Personality Assessment?

The 16-type assessments add two more dimensions to the four quadrant assessments, therefore they can be more accurate in the results. More accuracy should lead to better EQ and better relationships. The drawback is that unless you have studied and used these extensively, they are not as memorable as the four quadrant assessments, so they may not be as easy to use. This is especially true in teams with ten or more members.

How do 16-type Personality Assessments work?

The idea is that people have four pairs of traits. The assessment will ask questions around each pair and give you a rating on each pair. The result of (two choices) raised to (the fourth power) is 16 possible combinations.

What are the general details?

The ones that I'm aware of are computerized versions. The administrator will send you a link or code, you go on the computer and answer the questions, the administrator gets the results and shares them with you.

Myers-Briggs Type Indicator (MBTI)

The Myers-Briggs Type Indicator (commonly abbreviated MBTI[55]) was constructed by two Americans, Katharine Cook Briggs and her daughter Isabel Briggs Myers. The MBTI is based on the conceptual theory proposed by Swiss psychiatrist Carl Jung[56], who had speculated that people experience the world using four principal psychological functions – sensation, intuition, feeling, and thinking – and that one of these four functions is dominant for a person most of the time. The four categories (dimensions) are:
- Introversion/Extraversion (I/E)
- Sensing/Intuition (S/N)
- Thinking/Feeling (T/F)
- Judging/Perception (J/P)

Each person is said to have one preferred quality from each category, producing 16 unique types. Because of this, a survey that is based on the work by Jung is often called a "preferences assessment."

The MBTI has been used extensively in the corporate world and many people are major supporters. The drawback in use with large organizations is that the four letters are generally hard for non-proponents to remember, and therefore are not as easy to use as the DISC.

I have taken MBTI several times, and the issue that I have is that the assessment is designed to put you on one side of the dimension or the other. In other words, the dimension (Introversion vs. Extroversion, for example) is either one or the other, it is not a continuum. I happen to be one of those individuals that is almost exactly in the middle on this dimension. The times that I have taken the MBTI, I have been one point to either side, I'm never showing a firm preference for one or the other. This is my reality; I need and show a mixture of both.

One good site for MBTI related information is Personality Junkie[57]. You can sign up for their newsletter and a free personality type assessment.

---

[55] wikipedia.org/wiki/Myers%E2%80%93Briggs_Type_Indicator
[56] wikipedia.org/wiki/Carl_Jung
[57] personalityjunkie.com

Keirsey Temperament Sorter (KTS)

The Keirsey Temperament Sorter[58] (KTS) was created by David Keirsey. He expanded on the ancient study of temperament by Hippocrates and Plato. Keirsey divided the four temperaments into two categories (roles), each with two types (role variants). The resulting 16 types correlate with (but do not correspond to) the 16 personality types described by Briggs and Myers.

The type descriptions of Isabel Myers differ from the character descriptions of David Keirsey in several important ways:
- Myers primarily focused on how people think and feel; Keirsey focused more on behavior, which is directly observable.
- Myers' descriptions use a linear four-factor model; Keirsey's descriptions use a systems field theory model.
- Myers, following Jung's lead, emphasized the extraversion/introversion (expressive/attentive) dichotomy; Keirsey's model places greater importance on the sensing/intuition (concrete/abstract) dichotomy.
- Myers grouped types by 'function attitudes'; Keirsey, by temperament.

One issue that I see with the KTS is that it uses the same four letters as the MBTI. I could see that this could cause confusion with people who are familiar with one thinking that they are talking about the same thing with the people who are familiar with the other.

I have no direct experience with the KTS so I list this information here without additional comment.

---

[58] wikipedia.org/wiki/Keirsey_Temperament_Sorter

Chapter Eight: Enneagram

*The greatest risk any of us will take,
is to be seen as we are.
~~ Cinderella*

The Enneagram[59] is a model of the human psyche which is principally understood and taught as a typology of nine interconnected personality types[60]. The Enneagram has recently become very popular in Christian circles and seems to be getting a lot of attention. A Google search returns over six million results.

Why might you consider the Enneagram?

While the Enneagram is a personality assessment like the four-quadrant or 16-type assessments, the Enneagram leans more toward the nurture side of things, suggesting that types emerge as a response to early childhood experiences, according to Dr. A.J. Drenth in a blog post[61] on the Personality Junkie website.

How does the Enneagram work?

The Enneagram types are typically described in a more holistic or less structured manner than the Myers-Briggs types. Each type is assigned a nickname, which immediately imparts a holistic understanding (e.g., "The Peacemaker") of that type. This has the advantage of conveying a wealth of information in a single concept, even for Enneagram newcomers. A potential disadvantage, however, is that if a particular nickname fails to resonate with readers, they may quickly lose interest in learning about that type. Type nicknames also have the potential to overshadow worthwhile details and nuances contained in lengthier expositions. In short, there seems to be a trade-off between accuracy / analysis and the immediate sense of power and resonance engendered by a more holistic concept.

---

[59] wikipedia.org/wiki/Enneagram_of_Personality
[60] wikipedia.org/wiki/Personality_type
[61] personalityjunkie.com/12/myers-briggs-mbti-vs-enneagram

What are the general details?

The assessments that I've seen are administered via a computer and the results are a multi-page report.

I know several Professional Christian Coaches who use and recommend the Enneagram.

Some good places to get more information about the Enneagram:
- The Enneagram Institute[62]
- RHETI[63] - The Riso-Hudson[64] Enneagram Type Indicator, a free Enneagram assessment
- The FAST Enneagram Test[65], another free Enneagram assessment
- The IEQ9 enneagram report[66] gives a detailed report for individuals as well as teams.
- The Personality Junkie[67] website has details about the Enneagram and the MBTI.

I took the RHETI and my top two numbers were tied. The descriptions both seemed to fit me. This may be because I really am a combination personality, or it may be the precision of the RHETI test, or I might need to be coached in my Enneagram results.

To be fair, I have not spent that much time studying and learning about the Enneagram, so my information is limited.

---

[62] enneagraminstitute.com
[63] tests.enneagraminstitute.com
[64] wikipedia.org/wiki/Riso%E2%80%93Hudson_Enneagram_Type_Indicator
[65] enneagramtest.net
[66] integrative9.com/getyourtype
[67] personalityjunkie.com/enneagram-posts

Chapter Nine: EQ Assessments

*No one cares how much you know,
until they know how much you care.
~~ Theodore Roosevelt*

Why might you consider an EQ assessment?

Given that EQ is the basis of relationship, the hope would be that by taking an EQ assessment you would be able to see where you could improve, and perhaps the tool would give you some clues as to how to go about improving. This should improve your overall relationships.

Unfortunately, considering the number of books and articles on Emotional Intelligence, there are not a lot of assessments related to it that I have found.

Two organizations that specialize in Emotional Intelligence are:
- Genos International[68]. This organization has a great article on their website, "Which emotional intelligence assessment should I use[69]?"
- Six Seconds[70]. I have a Professional Christian Coaching friend that is Six Seconds certified. The available tools from Six Seconds are listed here[71].
- Positive Psychology has a good article[72] about Emotional Intelligence Tests.

I look forward to the opportunity to explore this exciting new area of assessments!

---

[68] genosinternational.com
[69] genosinternational.com/which-emotional-intelligence-assessment-should-i-use
[70] 6seconds.org
[71] 6seconds.org/tools/sei
[72] positivepsychology.com/emotional-intelligence-tests/

Chapter Ten: StrengthsFinder

"There is no more effective way to
empower people than to see each
person in terms of his or her strengths."
~~ Donald Clifton

(* In April 2018, I became a WeAlign Executive Coach, which relies heavily on the StrengthsFinder.)

Why might you consider the StrengthsFinder Assessment?

The StrengthsFinder gives you the most accurate view of yourself of any assessment I have seen out there on the market. You were not lumped into categories of billions or millions of other people, like a DISC or MBTI or Enneagram. You are unique and your StrengthsFinder assessment is unique, because it has 34 talents; for someone else to have the same top ten talents in the same order as you, the chance is 1 in 447 trillion. The StrengthsFinder gives you a perspective on how you are unique, and how and why you can work in your strengths. Once I went through the complete process, my life shifted dramatically for the better. I have seen multiple lives significantly improved when they applied what they learned through the process.

How does the StrengthsFinder Assessment work?

The StrengthsFinder is a theory and an assessment. The theory is:

> People are exponentially more productive, happy and motivated when their work aligns with their natural talents and strengths.

Gallup is the organization that manages and administers the CliftonStrengths[73] Assessment. The assessment ranks your 34 identified talents in order. A talent is a natural way of thinking, feeling or behaving that can be productively applied. You can tell something might be a talent for you if you seem to learn it **easily**, you do it with **excellence**, you really **enjoy** doing it, or you gain **energy** by doing it.

---

[73] gallup.com/cliftonstrengths/en/home.aspx

The foundation of a strength is a talent. A talent becomes a strength through **skill, knowledge,** and **experience.**

What are the general details?

What I'm calling the StrengthsFinder has had several names in its history:
- CliftonStrengths (current name since 2015)
- Clifton StrengthsFinder (official name before 2015)
- Gallup StrengthsFinder (unofficial name)

My StrengthsFinder Story, part 1

For many years, I had a love/hate relationship with the StrengthsFinder. I loved, grasped, understood, and appreciated the **theory** of the StrengthsFinder, which is that you should focus on your strengths instead of your weaknesses. Intuitively to me, this made a lot of sense.

However, I disliked — let's just say hated — the actual assessment itself, because it was so different from all the other assessments, and because they did not give you complete results, only the top five. The books I read about it listed over 30 strengths, and I would look over those, and wonder "why don't I have this", or "why do I have that one rather than this one?" It just seemed so random and incomplete.

StrengthsFinder has 34 different talents. The assessment that you take results in your order, from 1 to 34. However, most people only get the top five results. Between 2004 and 2013, I took the StrengthsFinder assessment four times. In all cases I only got my top five, and from assessment to assessment they were never the same. I would have maybe two from the previous assessment were still there, but they weren't in the same position or order. Frankly, because of this lack of repeatability, I did not think the assessment was very good.

My StrengthsFinder Story, part 2

However, I kept hearing fantastic results of other coaches that were using the StrengthsFinder. I kept an open mind and looked for an opportunity to find out more. In 2016, I decided to take the PCCI StrengthsFinder course with Brent O'Bannon[74]. (Brent was the very first ever Gallup certified strength coach.)

I took the assessment and for the first time got my "Full 34" results and not just my top five. This was a very good thing — and a very bad thing. It turned out on that assessment that competition was my number one strength. This does not fit me at all. It had never shown up anywhere in my top five before! And intuitively, I could not see any history in my past of competition the way it was described. There were times that I was competitive, but most of the time I was more cooperative than competitive. What was going on?

If you look at my timeline of what happened in 2016 in Chapter 2, you will see that it was a very big transition year for me. I got divorced, and I went to part-time in my IT career, and I was setting up my coaching business. At the time I took the assessment, I was under a lot of stress. There were several other talents that were out of order as well.

While I got a lot out of Brent's class about the StrengthsFinder, the history, how to use it, and a deeper understanding of what each strength was… it just didn't work for me with my results. It wasn't useful for me. I put it back on the shelf. That is, until…

---

[74] brentobannon.com/

My StrengthsFinder Story, part 3 — the WeAlign SAP

In 2018, I started meeting with a group of coaches in a Peer Mastermind. One of those coaches, Pete Cafarchio[75], was a WeAlign[76] Certified Coach. As we would discuss things in our peer group, he would also mention some of the results that he was getting with his clients based on the WeAlign Strengths Alignment Process, or SAP[77]. I was intrigued and set up a one-to-one meeting with Pete to find out more information. He explained the process, and I committed to go through it. However, because of my experience with my 2016 results, we decided that I would redo the StrengthsFinder assessment. This was a major turning point in my relationship with the StrengthsFinder.

This time the assessment results fit me so much better. And while being coached through the WeAlign process by Pete, I understood how to use and apply those strengths in my life. I immediately saw major changes that I needed to make, and one of those changes was to become a WeAlign Certified Coach myself.

I started the certification process[78] in January 2019. This involves getting through their training, taking a test, and then getting some clients to go through the process. I found the process straightforward, well documented, easy to apply, and very practically useful for the client. (Perhaps I had some advantage, since I already had so much coach training.)

I have seen this SAP process literally change lives, and everyone who has gone through it has indicated that it has been very impactful to them on a personal level. So much so, that in my marketing I call the process "StrengthsFinder On Steroids."

Other Testimonials

Here are a couple of testimonials from clients I coached through the WeAlign SAP during this time.

---

[75] petecoaching.com
[76] wealigncoaching.com
[77] wealigncoaching.com/services
[78] wealigncoaching.com/for-coaches

"The StrengthsFinder process confirmed my vague awareness about using a strength unconsciously and gave me the confidence to stop wasting energy second guessing myself. This opened up the power to believe in myself and in my strengths to be who God created me to be regardless of others expectations."
~~ Chuck Couch

"I quit swimming upstream! While doing the SF program I learned several things:
- I learned so much about who I am and what I am naturally good at.
- I learned that I had been trying to fit myself in a box based on other people's expectations of me.
- I learned that while I thought I was good at some things, they really didn't come natural to me.
- I learned that by focusing on what I am naturally good at, I can be exponentially better at what I do."

~~ SAM Morrison

SAM was nice enough to record a video testimonial for me about what she got out of the process. It is available on my website[79].

In the last couple of years, I have really understood the power and the potential in the StrengthsFinder, and currently it is my favorite assessment tool. The StrengthsFinder has a depth and a uniqueness about it that helps you understand who you are at a core level.

---

[79] coachdale.com/sfos

Chapter Eleven: Spiritual Gifts

*Just as each one has received a gift, use it
to serve others, as good stewards of the varied
grace of God. ~~ 1 Peter 4:10*

Why might you consider a Spiritual Gifts Assessment?

A spiritual gift[80] is an endowment or extraordinary power given by the Holy Spirit. These are supernatural graces which individual Christians need to fulfill the mission of the Church and the good of others.

As a Christian, it is important to understand your place within the Christian community, and the gift(s) that have been given to you, for service to your fellow believers.

How do Spiritual Gifts Assessments work?

Spiritual gift assessments take the list of gifts from the New Testament Bible found in Romans 12, 1 Corinthians 12, Ephesians 4, and 1 Peter 4 and put questions around each gift. Typically you rate yourself on that question and you (or the computer) add up the results. The gifts with the highest ratings are then your top gift(s).

What are the general details?

Wikipedia has a great page on spiritual gifts[81].

For assessments, I have seen both paper and computerized versions. The paper versions are typically very simple, with seven or fewer gifts and ten or fewer questions. Computerized versions typically list 12 or 14 gifts and often contain over 100 questions. These assessments may produce a detailed report or may only give you the gift name(s), and a standard chart to look up the results.

Here are a few spiritual gift assessments that I have found online:

---

[80] wikipedia.org/wiki/Spiritual_gift
[81] wikipedia.org/wiki/Spiritual_gift

- Church Growth Spiritual Gifts Survey[82]
- Spiritual Gifts Test[83]
- Adventist Spiritual Gifts Assessment[84]

I haven't taken these, so I will not comment on how good or reliable they are.

Many churches have their own preference for which assessment, so check with your local church. My church, Frisco Bible Church[85], has its own version which is similar to the ones above.

---

[82] gifts.churchgrowth.org/spiritual-gifts-survey
[83] spiritualgiftstest.com/spiritual-gifts-test-landing
[84] youth.adventist.org/Resources/Spiritual-Gifts-Assessment
[85] friscobible.com

Chapter Twelve: Combo

*Nothing comes from nothing, Thieflet; no story comes
from nowhere; new stories are born from old--
it is the new combinations that make them new.*
~~ Salman Rushdie, *Haroun and the Sea of Stories*

Why might you consider a Combo Assessment?

A combination (combo) assessment combines more than one type of assessment into a single instrument. As such, they can be good value for the money and time invested. If you are part of a group or organization that uses one of these, or if your Coach is certified in a particular assessment, it can make a lot of sense to participate.

How do Combo Assessments work?

Each section on the end result is usually assessed in a separate section of the assessment. Most of these are computerized. Typically you will end up with a multi-page report with the results.

What are the general details?

See each of the individual items below.

COREmap

(* I became COREmap certified in 2008. I administered my last COREmap in 2012.)

I put the COREmap[86] in the combo assessments because it has three parts:
- Part 1 is a four-quadrant type assessment (i.e. DISC or temperament).
- Part 2 is a preference assessment similar to a light Myers-Briggs, using three pairs instead of four.
- Part 3 is called the Effectiveness Graph. This is a chart which I have not seen in any other assessment. The Effectiveness Graph measures how well you are doing in each of the four quadrants.

I first took the COREmap in 2005 through the Pathways[87] organization where I was volunteering. Over the next couple of years, I took this assessment another three or four times. My results on Parts 1 and 2 were remarkably consistent. It was interesting, though, that I showed improvement on the Part 3.

I do like the names that COREmap uses for the four quadrants (and their corresponding DISC type):
- C - Commander   (D - Dominant)
- O - Organizer   (C - Conscientiousness)
- R - Relator   (S - Steadiness)
- E - Entertainer   (I - Influence)

Not only are the names more directly related to the observed personalities, but they are also easier for most people to remember.

Note that while DISC often goes clockwise around the quadrants, CORE goes the opposite direction, counterclockwise.

Because of using both temperaments and preferences, and the presence of the Effectiveness Graph, COREmap is a very good instrument. I have no problem continuing to recommend the COREmap.

---

[86] coremap.com
[87] see: Pathways, page 72

RightPath

The RightPath[88] has two assessments, the RightPath 4 and RightPath 6. I placed the RightPath in the combo section because of the two assessments.

The RightPath 4 and 6 assessments are administered via computer and a 12 to 14 page report is produced with each.

The RightPath has a presence in the business environment. I was exposed to it through two courses at Professional Christian Coaching Institute. I took it first in 2011 and then in 2014, and my results were reasonably consistent.

The RightPath 4 plots your behavior as four pairs of traits which give 16 possible results, but unlike the MBTI[89] it gives you a range and lets you see just how far your preference for that trait is from the center.

The RightPath 6 plots your behavior as six pairs of traits which give 64 possible results.

I found that in a team environment, sharing RightPath 4 and 6 results improved understanding for most people.

---

[88] rightpath.com/site
[89] see: MBTI, page 44

SHAPE

SHAPE has been used in several Christian organizations, and we use it at Frisco Bible Church. SHAPE is an acronym for:

- S - Spiritual Gifts
- H - Heart - this is your Passion, what you LOVE to do
- A - Abilities - these are the things you CAN do, your strengths
- P - Personality - typically a flavor of DISC
- E - Experiences - what you've experienced

Frisco Bible Church has developed their own version of this assessment.

Apparently, SHAPE was first used or popularized at Saddleback Church.

This on-line version of SHAPE[90] seems to be very similar to the one from Frisco Bible Church with which I am familiar.

---

[90] freeshapetest.com

Chapter Thirteen: Other Assessments

*Our thoughts and imaginations are the
only real limits to our possibilities.
~~ Orison Swett Marden*

As I was researching assessments, I was referred to several, which I have not had time to research. I list them here just to give you a flavor of the assessments that are on the market. I do not make any statements as to the usefulness of these.

- The Five Factor Model[91].
- *LINKED Quick Guide to Personalities: Maximizing Life Connections One Link at a Time*[92]. This appears to be a four-quadrant assessment.
- SDS Self Directed Search[93]. This seems to be a combination assessment which matches your personality with professional occupations.
- MAPP (Motivational Appraisal Personal Potential)[94]. Another career location assessment.
- PLACE[95]. This is a combination test which includes Personality, Learning spiritual gifts, Abilities, Connecting passion with ministry, and Experiences. It sounds very similar to SHAPE[96].
- Method Teaming[97].
- KLLP Kendall Life Languages Profile[98].
- 12 Driving Forces[99].
- Emotional Quotient[100].

---

[91] wikipedia.org/wiki/Big_Five_personality_traits
[92] smile.amazon.com/dp/1946708259
[93] wikipedia.org/wiki/John_L._Holland
[94] assessment.com
[95] placeministries.org/an-individual.html
[96] see: SHAPE, page 59
[97] methodteaming.com
[98] lifelanguages.com
[99] 12drivingforces.ttisi.com
[100] talentsmart.com/products/emotional-intelligence-appraisal.php

- Birkman[101]. I have actually taken a form of the Birkman. It is another combo assessment and there were interesting aspects to it.
- Grip-Birkman[102]. This "combo of combos" adds a spiritual gift assessment to the Birkman.
- Kolbe[103]. "Kolbe measures your instinctive way of doing things and the result is called your MO (method of operation)."
- Via Character Strengths[104]. At first glance, this appears to be similar to the Gallup CliftonStrengths, but with 24 "Character Strengths" instead of 34 talents.

And still more!

Every time I look up an assessment that I think I already know, I find something new, but I also find links to even more assessments. I easily found the assessments above as I was researching the ones for this book that I had already determined to write about.

At the end of the day, a good understanding of the major categories:
- Four-Quadrant
- 16-Type
- Strengths
- Combo

will serve to help you understand how assessments fit into common practice, or how they are different/unique.

---

[101] birkman.com
[102] gripbirkman.ca/grip-birkman-method.html
[103] kolbe.com
[104] viacharacter.org

Section Three:

IDENTITY TOOLS

This section contains the tools other than assessments (experiences, people, and organizations) that I know about for helping you in your identity journey.

In an atlas, this would be everything that is not in the previous section.

Each tool has its own chapter so that it will be easy to locate in the table of contents.

Chapter Fourteen: Writing / Journaling / Diaries

*Be who you are and say what you feel because those
who mind don't matter and those who matter don't mind.
~~ Dr. Seuss*

Why might you consider journaling?

According to Intermountain Healthcare[105] and other internet resources, journaling:
- Reduces stress.
- Improves immune function.
- Keeps memory sharp.
- Boosts mood.
- Strengthens emotional functions.

Given the benefits and the low cost, if you haven't tried journaling before, it's worthwhile to attempt it. While it's definitely not for everyone, I know several people who have had tremendous breakthroughs while journaling.

How does journaling work?

Writing[106] is communication through words on paper or a screen.

Journaling[107] is used in several different contexts, but for our purposes we'll concentrate on two:
- Writing in a diary[108], which could be paper or electronic, private or public. Blogs can be one form of public electronic diaries.
- Writing therapy[109], in which writing one's feelings gradually eases emotional trauma.

---

[105] intermountainhealthcare.org/blogs/topics/live-well/2018/07/5-powerful-health-benefits-of-journaling
[106] dictionary.com/browse/writing
[107] wikipedia.org/wiki/Journaling
[108] wikipedia.org/wiki/Diary
[109] wikipedia.org/wiki/Writing_therapy

Many studies (over 200) have shown benefits to the process of writing, including:
- the fact that often writing something down allows the brain to stop dwelling on that thought;
- the writer can perceive experiences more clearly;
- and it even boosts the immune system in many tests.

Journaling can also be applied to the spoken word; with the voice recorders that are built into most smartphones today, you can talk your journal instead of type or write it. This can be effective for verbal processors.

The important part is getting your thoughts and feelings out of your brain.

Thought question(s): have you journaled? Was it beneficial?

Chapter Fifteen: Affirmations

> I think, therefore I am.[110]
> ~~ René Descartes

Why might you consider affirmations?

Once an affirmation is created, it only takes a few seconds or minutes to say/review them. Even if you do this multiple times per day, it is still a very effective use of your time considering the benefits of clearer thought, better self-identity, and positive thinking.

How do affirmations work?

Affirmations in the sense of identity tools are positive statements made for yourself. Wikipedia lists multiple[111] uses for affirmation, but let's concentrate on these three:
- Affirmative prayer[112], a form of prayer that focuses on a positive outcome.
- Self-affirmation[113], the psychological process of re-affirming personal values to protect self-identity.
- Affirmations (New Age)[114], the practice of positive thinking in New Age terminology.

The New Age practice has popularized the concept of affirmations in recent years, but positive thought goes back centuries. Check out the Apostle Paul in Philippians:

> Finally brothers and sisters, whatever is true, whatever is honorable, whatever is just, whatever is pure, whatever is lovely, whatever is commendable—if there is any moral excellence and if there is anything praiseworthy—dwell on these things. ~~ Philippians 4:8, CSB

---

[110] wikipedia.org/wiki/Cogito,_ergo_sum
[111] wikipedia.org/wiki/Affirmation
[112] wikipedia.org/wiki/Affirmative_prayer
[113] wikipedia.org/wiki/Self-affirmation
[114] wikipedia.org/wiki/Affirmations_(New_Age)

Returning to the points raised in RARE Leadership[115], if you make daily affirmations a habit, you will be helping the fast-track system to continue to function even under difficulties. This will keep your identity strong and consistent.

Thought question(s): do you have a set of affirmations for yourself? If you do, what could you improve? If you don't, what would it take for you to try it for 30 days?

---

[115] see: RARE Leadership, page 30

Chapter Sixteen: Music

*Music is a piece of art
that goes in the ears,
straight to the heart.
~~ Unknown*

Music has a power to go straight to your emotions. I am very careful about the kind of music I consume. As an old computer programmer, I learned early about the "Garbage In, Garbage Out" (GIGO[116]) principle. Therefore, I primarily listen to Christian music, and I check the lyrics to make sure they fit with my beliefs.

Music is a big part of my journey. I've never been a musician, I don't play instruments, I don't sing other than casually, and I've never studied the process of creating music. I used to say that the only instrument that I could play was a CD player! Now, I can play Spotify, Apple Music, and YouTube. My options have expanded!

I've always appreciated music. Music puts me in touch with my emotions, my sense of feeling and wonder. Since the mid 2000's I've been creating playlists of music, and since 2011 I've been creating annual playlists of my favorite Christian songs from the year. I have published these playlists with links to Spotify, Apple Music, and YouTube on my website. They are part of my gift[117] to the world.

Thought question(s): what kind of music do you like? Are you intentional about the kind and amount of music that you consume?

---

[116] dictionary.com/browse/gigo?s=t
[117] coachdale.com/playlists

Chapter Seventeen: Books

So many books, so little time.
~~Frank Zappa

The following is a list of books that I'm aware of, that have a good focus on identity.

RARE Leadership[118] by Dr. Marcus Warner and Dr. Jim Wilder - covered previously[119].

Halftime: Moving from Success to Significance[120] by Bob Buford.

Cure for the Common Life[121] by Max Lucado. Max Lucado gives you tools and steps to find and live in your sweet spot, and your identity is a big part of that.

Wild at Heart[122] by John Eldredge.

The Bible — covers identity as well as a few (okay, a LOT of) other topics. Very worthwhile studying.

Books that touch on identity, but are focused on other subjects:

The Dream Giver[123] by Bruce Wilkinson

---

[118] smile.amazon.com/Rare-Leadership-Uncommon-Increasing-Engagement/dp/0802414540
[119] see: RARE Leadership, page 30
[120] smile.amazon.com/Halftime-Changing-Your-Success-Significance-ebook/dp/B000SG9IUE/
[121] smile.amazon.com/Cure-Common-Life-Max-Lucado/dp/0849947081
[122] smile.amazon.com/Wild-Heart-Revised-Updated-Discovering/dp/1400200393
[123] smile.amazon.com/Dream-Giver-Bruce-Wilkinson/dp/159052201X

The Purpose Driven Life[124] by Rick Warren

The Search for Significance[125] by Robert S. McGee

Living Forward[126] by Michael Hyatt and Daniel Harkavy

2 Chairs[127] by Bob Beaudine

There are likely hundreds more, but those are the ones on my physical and digital bookshelf which I recommend.

Thought question: which book has had the biggest impact on you?

---

[124] smile.amazon.com/Purpose-Driven-Life-What-Earth/dp/031033750X
[125] smile.amazon.com/Search-Significance-Seeing-Worth-Through/dp/0849944244
[126] smile.amazon.com/Living-Forward-Proven-Plan-Drifting-ebook/dp/B012H10GBW
[127] smile.amazon.com/Chairs-Secret-That-Changes-Everything/dp/1683972538

Chapter Eighteen: Podcasts

*What distinguishes radio from TV is the intimacy.
What distinguishes a podcast from radio is that
it's intimacy plus, because you've chosen it
and it's literally in your ears. ~~ Olly Mann*

Although there are likely some podcasts that focus on identity — there seem to be multiple podcasts for every other topic under the sun — I don't know of any that specifically focus on identity.

Many podcasts are more general purpose, and will often touch on aspects of identity, but certainly not in every episode and often not dealing with it in a full episode, but only as a subset of the whole theme. Here are a few that I know of that deal with identity often.

Professional Christian Coaching Today[128] by Chris McCluskey and Kim Avery.
This podcast focuses on coaching, which is an awesome tool for helping someone find their identity. They often talk about different kinds of assessments, and they interview people with different specialties, some of which are focused on identity work.

Eternal Leadership Podcast[129] by John Ramstead.
This podcast is focused around Christian leadership. As such, the identity topic often comes up. You can get to the podcast via the Eternal Leadership website: http://eternalleadership.com/blog/

One Eternal Leadership podcast in particular from July 2015[130] had an awesome affirmation read by the guest.

Dynamic Destiny Radio[131] by Pete Cafarchio. While focused more around where you are going, instead of who you are, Coach Pete often talks about identity aspects in order to help you along the "where am I going" journey. And after all, everything is connected, right?

---

[128] professionalchristiancoaching.com/podcast
[129] eternalleadership.com/blog
[130] eternalleadership.com/063
[131] www.transformationtalkradio.com/show-details/dynamic-destiny-radio-with-coach-pete-cafarchio-unpack-your-powerful-potential,246.html

Thought question: which podcast(s) do you regularly follow?

Chapter Nineteen: Experiential-Based Retreats

> God uses broken people like you and me
> to rescue broken people like you and me.
> ~~Eddie Cortes

Why might you consider experiential-based retreats?

These seminars provide an extremely focused retreat around whatever issue they address. Because of the focus, you can make a lot of progress in a very rapid fashion. As a side benefit, because these are all done in groups of people with groups of people, there are inherent relational and EQ improvements.

How do experiential-based retreats work?

So… what are they? The ones I'm aware of that will really help you with the "who are you?" question — well, to call them seminars or trainings is something of an injustice. They are more than and different from most seminars, trainings, workshops, or retreats. I'm choosing to call them "retreats" because that word conveys the clearest sense of any of them, although all of them have been applied at one time or another.

The basic theory is that most of your issues were caused by other people, whether they are currently in your life or not. To heal from this, you need to be around people — you won't heal on your own.

The retreats that I've experienced are significant and help you change your life and discover aspects of who you are.

I have participated, and volunteered for, several experiential-based retreats. These retreats are typically held over multiple days over a weekend, and some of them require stays at various sites or hotels. To do the full training with all parts, some extend over multiple weekends, sometimes several months.

I'll discuss and provide more details about the ones I know. If I've heard of others that are similar, I'll include them.

Experiential-Based Retreats: Pathways

(* *I attended Pathways beginning in April 2004, and volunteered extensively from 2005 to 2009.*)

Pathways[132] is a Las Colinas, Texas-based, global non-profit organization providing training to help build lives of significance and communities of hope.

Pathways' belief is each person deserves a chance to live a life by design rather than default: any circumstance can be overcome; all wounds can be healed; and no two people's paths are the same. The experiential trainings are uniquely individualized. Each trainee identifies what they want and how they can make positive changes to achieve it.

The Core Training program is the successor to self-empowerment trainings created by Dr. Phil McGraw in 1985.

According to fairly common and consistent discussion among Pathways graduates, in the late 1990's/early 2000's, Dr. Phil was getting involved with Oprah Winfrey, at first through the (in)famous Amarillo Beef Trial[133] in 1998, then on her show, then helping Dr. Phil get his own show. During this period, Dr. Phil had turned Pathways over to the people who were the main facilitators. At some point, these people started asking permission (or not) to take the syllabus and make their own changes, and they went out and created 'Pathways-like' trainings. I know of two (The Road Adventure[134] and Barnabas Journey[135]), and I've heard there are several more (Discovery may be one of them). I'll describe the Pathways program in general, and then I'll list the changes for The Road Adventure. While I know that Barnabas was a Pathways spin-off, I haven't attended or volunteered for it, so I won't comment any further.

Pathways accepts all religious beliefs and does not support one belief over another in the training. However, one of their core beliefs is

---

[132] pathwayscoretraining.org
[133] texastribune.org/2018/01/10/time-oprah-winfrey-beefed-texas-cattle-industry
[134] theroadadventure.org
[135] barnabasjourney.org

unconditional love. Many volunteers profess Christian beliefs, but not all.

Trainings are currently held only in the Dallas, Texas area.

The full Pathways program is five multi-day retreats. All except the second of the five are Friday night, all day Saturday, and Sunday until 6:00 pm. The second retreat starts at noon on Wednesday, is all day Thursday, Friday, and Saturday, and Sunday until 6:00 pm. These are typically held in a hotel with several training rooms, and you are required to stay in the hotel during the training. The first and second are typically scheduled during the same month. The third, fourth, and fifth trainings are best done consecutively during the next three months.

Retail cost per their website as of January 2020 for all five retreats is $3,625. Discounts are sometimes available.

As you can see, this is a significant investment of time and money. However, I have seen lives radically changed for the better through the program. And it made a significant impact on me. For one, I learned more about myself in those five trainings than I had in 50 years before. I gained an immediate EQ boost. And I made major strides on my journey to my current self-identity.

Experiential-Based Retreats: The Road Adventure

(* *I attended The Road Adventure beginning in January 2018, started volunteering in July 2018, and still volunteer with them when I can.*)

As stated previously, The Road Adventure[136] was a spin-off from Pathways in the early 2000 timeframe. It was created to bring an explicitly Christian aspect to the Pathways training.

It also provides shorter training with less cost. A hotel stay is not required by the program.

There are three parts for the full Road Adventure:
- Part 1 - Friday evening, all day Saturday, Sunday from 2:00 to 6:00 pm
- Part 2 - Thursday evening, Friday evening, all day Saturday, Sunday from 2:00 to 6:00 pm
- Part 3 - Friday evening, all day Saturday, Sunday from 2:00 to 6:00 pm

Typically Part 1 is one month, and Part 2 is the next month. Part 3 is scheduled less frequently, typically there will be two Part 1/Part 2 classes before there is a Part 3 class.

Retail cost per the web site in January 2020 is $549 plus online registration fees. Discounts are often available, and all U.S. military personnel and all first responders (active or veterans) (and their spouses) can attend all three weekends of The Road for free!

Trainings are currently held only in the Dallas, Texas area.

I went through the program in January 2018 because I was blocking myself from dating and didn't know what was causing it. Also, I had heard that it was a Christian program and was less expensive than Pathways and I wanted to see it for myself. I discovered my issue, and found a good program that I fully support.

Depending on what you need, what kind of things you are struggling with, and your spiritual beliefs, The Road Adventure can deliver 70%+

---

[136] theroadadventure.org

of the Pathways experience in less than 20% of the cost and about half the time.

Experiential-Based Retreats: The Walk to Emmaus

(* I attended The Walk to Emmaus in October 2006, started volunteering in 2010, and still volunteer with them when I can. In addition, as I write this in January 2020, I am serving on the Dallas Emmaus Board of Directors for the Walk to Emmaus.)

The Walk to Emmaus[137] is a spiritual retreat. The name is taken from The Bible in Luke 24:13-35. It is a world-wide phenomenon, with trainings in all geographic areas. Most weekends there will be several Walks to Emmaus being held somewhere in the world.

Just to be clear, there's not a lot of physical walking, the walk in the title is referring to your spiritual walk.

Emmaus is open to members of any Christian denominations. Emmaus is for the development of Christian leaders who:
- Are members of a local church.
- Have a desire to strengthen their spiritual lives.
- May have unanswered questions about their faith.
- Understand that being a Christian involves responsibility.
- Are willing to dedicate their everyday lives to God in an ongoing manner.

With the recommendation of their local pastor and a sponsor, they can apply to go on the Walk to Emmaus.

The Walk to Emmaus starts Thursday evening and continues until Sunday at 6:00 pm. It is a very structured program, controlled by The Upper Room[138]. The cost is determined by the local community. For the Dallas Emmaus[139] community, the cost is $220 as of January 2020.

The Walk consists of 15 talks around Christian subjects and is a short course in Christian theology. Walks are held for men and women separately. Most people who attend a Walk come out with a renewed sense of who they are in Christ and a desire to use their gifts to serve others.

---

[137] emmaus.upperroom.org
[138] upperroom.org
[139] dallasemmaus.org

I understand, but don't know for certain, that "Tres Dias[140]" (Spanish for Three Days) is very similar to The Walk to Emmaus.

Thought question(s): have you been on any kind of retreat? What was the result?

---

[140] tresdias.org

Chapter Twenty: Coaching

*Counsel in a person's heart is deep water;
but a person of understanding draws it out.
~~ Proverbs 20:5, CSB*

Why might you consider coaching?

Coaching is all about getting results faster than you would on your own. The client and the coach form a partnership to accomplish goals that are meaningful to the client, and then overcome the obstacles and resistance that invariably get in the way.

Background on coaching

Coaching is a helping industry that is not currently regulated in the United States, and thus the definition of coaching is open to interpretation.

Dictionary.com[141] lists 11 nouns, three verbs, and an adverb — and none of them meet the definition of a coach as defined by the International Coach Federation[142] (ICF), which is what I mean in this chapter:

> Coaching[143] is an interactive process that helps individuals and organizations to develop more rapidly and produce more satisfying results. Coaches work with clients in all areas including business, career, finances, health and relationships. As a result of coaching, clients set better goals, take more action, make better decisions, and more fully use their natural strengths.
>
> Professional coaches are trained to listen and observe, to customize their approach to the individual client's needs, and to elicit solutions and strategies from the client. They believe that

---

[141] dictionary.com
[142] coachfederation.org
[143] apps.coachfederation.org/eweb/DynamicPage.aspx?Site=icf&WebKey=6755006e-d18d-45c0-8024-8f479a3dedd8

the client is naturally creative and resourceful and that the coach's job is to provide support to enhance the skills, resources, and creativity that the client already has. While the coach provides feedback and an objective perspective, the client is responsible for taking the steps to produce the results he or she desires. Coaching does not focus directly on relieving psychological pain or treating cognitive or emotional disorders.

> Coach. (noun) 1. a large, horse-drawn, four-wheeled carriage, usually enclosed.
> ~~ Coach[144] at Dictionary.com

Let's go back to the original definition of the word coach:

Actually, this definition is a good metaphor for the ICF role of a coach. In essence, the coach is a vehicle that will take you from one place to the next, without dictating your path or direction. ICF coaching is often referred to as "non-directive coaching" because the coach does not have an agenda and does not tell the client what to do. The coach is not the expert.

Expert Coaching

In contrast to the ICF-style non-directive coaching, there are "expert" coaches. Many people, when they hear "coach" or "coaching", think of athletic coaches, which is one type of expert. Expert coaches know a particular area/subject and provide advice and direction. This is not limited to athletics. There are coaches that come into a business with a certain focus (for example, improving the sales team), and they can be highly directive. Coaches can come in to implement a new system such as Entrepreneur Operating System (EOS) or SalesForce, and those have best practices that dictate what should and should not be done.

Experts tend to exist in Business, Dating, Financial, Health and Wellness, Sports, and Vocals. In many ways, I think of coaches like this as more Consultants[145] — they have the expert "how-to", "best practice" information and their role is to come alongside and help you implement.

---

[144] dictionary.com/browse/coach?s=t
[145] wikipedia.org/wiki/Consultant

This is not to say that all coaches in these areas always take the expert approach. In many cases, it is not a "one or the other" but more of a "both and" blended approach.

ICF Coaching

In the ICF world, the coach is NOT the expert. The client is the expert in their life and business, they have the wisdom inside them to deal with the situation, and the coach is there to bring that internal wisdom out.

A great way to think about this is to imagine two chairs, and two people. In consulting and expert-type coaching, the client and the coach are in chairs setting side by side and they are both looking outward, at the problem that they are together trying to solve.

In Counseling, the two chairs are facing each other. The client has the problem "inside them" and is focused on either the counselor or they are focusing internally, while the counselor is focused on the client, and is diagnosing the problem and how to deal with it.

In Coaching, the client's chair is facing out toward the problem. The coach is focused on the client, and is focused on asking the client questions that will help them solve their own problem.

Christian Coaching

Christian Coaching is a subset of regular coaching that brings a Christian perspective to the coaching. A great example of this is the key coaching verse at the top of this chapter, Proverbs 20:5.

There is a wonderful episode on the Professional Christian Coaching podcast site titled "What is Professional Christian Coaching[146]". This episode goes into a lot of details about Coaching, Professional Coaching, and Professional Christian Coaching. Details about what it is, and what it is not. If you are interested in getting a solid foundation

---

[146] professionalchristiancoaching.com/128-encore-episode-what-is-professional-christian-coaching

in this area, this particular podcast episode will go a long way to filling any gaps. Highly recommended.

Hiring a Coach

If you are considering finding and hiring a coach, I suggest you do a bit of research. The links above provide good starting points. These are some of the questions that I believe you need to settle for yourself:

- Does my coach need to be credentialed in coaching? If so, which credential is important?
- Do I want a coach who has a lot of experience, or can I trust someone who is just starting out?
- Do I want a coach who specializes in the niche where my issue exists?
- How much am I willing to pay? -versus- How important is it for me to solve my problem?
- Do I have a great relationship (or feel like I can develop one) with this person?
- Is this a person I enjoy spending time with?
- Is this a person I can trust?
- Do they offer any type of free (or low-cost) session so I can see if we are compatible? (Most professional coaches do offer some type of initial session.)

At the end of the day, you want to be comfortable and trust the coach you are working with.

Thought question(s): have you ever been coached by an ICF coach? If so, what were your results? If not, does this sound like something you might find useful?

Chapter Twenty-One: Spiritual Growth

> All of us fail, but this
> doesn't mean we are failures.
> ~~ Robert McGee, The Search
> For Significance Workbook

Why might you consider spiritual growth?

As Christians, the Bible calls us in various places to grow in Christ. One good reference:

> Like newborn infants, desire the pure milk
> of the word, so that you may grow up into
> your salvation. ~~ 1 Peter 2:2, CSB

Spiritual Growth References

I was hesitant to even include this chapter in the book. After all, entire series of books have been written on the topic of spiritual growth. Thousands of years of Christianity have helped develop it. Millions of people.

But to leave out such an important topic would be cowardly. So, while I can't claim to do this topic justice, I can at least provide some starting points for your journey.

There are a lot of different definitions of spiritual growth and spiritual formation. The Wikipedia article[147] points you to many. There are reasons for this:
- It's a VERY big topic.
- There are a great number of perspectives.
- It's a very individual journey — what works great for one person doesn't work at all for another.

Let's use the One80 Life[148] Lens to identify the places to focus on our spiritual growth.

---

[147] wikipedia.org/wiki/Spiritual_formation
[148] see: One80 Life, page 19

Connection with God

To improve our connection with God, we have to (a) know who God is, and (b) spend time with Him sharing our thoughts and comprehending His.

The best place to get to know God is to study His word, the Bible. I credit most of my spiritual growth over the years to the fact that I read the Bible (almost) every day. I'm on a Bible reading plan where I read through the entire Bible every year. A Google search for "Bible Reading Plans" returns 72 million results, so there's likely a plan that works for you. There are plans that will take you through the Bible in three years instead of one. There are plans that will take you through only the New Testament — if you haven't read the Bible consistently, this might be a good place to start.

After the Bible, there are tons of other resources to help you get to know God. You can take courses in theology (the study of God), read other books (being sure to compare their wisdom against the Bible), refer to Bible dictionaries and concordances, talk with other believers, participate in study groups, and many more.

Reading and studying the Bible will not only increase your knowledge of God but also reveal His thoughts and will in general. To know His thoughts and will for you personally, you need to spend time with Him, and that is done through prayer and meditation, including spending time not only talking to Him, but also listening for what he is telling you. A great book on this subject, one that helped me tremendously, is 2 *Chairs*[149] by Bob Beaudine, although there are likely hundreds of others out there.

Healthy Connection with Others

Remember the "Smooth Stones[150]" concept in the Chapter Four: Connections chapter? We all become better and more mature when we interact with each other and knock off the rough edges. This is not to say the process is smooth, as it is often painful, but the result is smooth and beautiful.

---

[149] smile.amazon.com/Chairs-Secret-That-Changes-Everything/dp/1683972538
[150] see: Smooth Stones, page 22

Given that, it is absolutely critical to your spiritual growth that you be in some form of Christian community. Typically this is a local church, but there are other alternatives as well — Bible studies at work or in your (non-church) community, Christian Business groups, even CEO Mastermind groups like Convene[151]. These communities provide support, accountability, and opportunities for growth. Find one or more that fit you and get plugged in!

One word of warning: if you are in a church or other community that is NOT encouraging growth, then find some other method. It might mean joining some other group in addition that does focus on growth, it might mean listening to sermons from other churches or reading books, it might even mean that you need to find a different church or community. I'm certainly not advocating the "church shopping" mentality that some people have, church is not designed for your entertainment and consumption — church is ultimately responsible for helping you become more like Jesus and how He created you to be.

A good church or community will not only help you with healthy connection with others, but can also provide hints and helps around the connection with God and the connection with your true self.

Connection with True Self

Without connection, we are without hope, belief, or purpose. A young person (under age 4) is very connected with themselves, but as we grow older, we lose that connection. Perhaps you are judged, or you get in trouble for the way you express yourself. Any negative experience can cause you to suppress your natural self, so you become afraid to be authentic. You lose that sense of self-worth.

Often, it is a process to undo the layers of damage and doubt that have accumulated over the years.

In one sense, this entire book gives ideas and suggestions for resources to help you improve your connection with your true self.

---

[151] convenenow.com

One book in particular that has helped me and millions of others in this area is *The Search For Significance* [152] by Robert McGee. This book helped me get rid of some of the thoughts and feelings of unworthiness that I had picked up as a child. Highly recommended.

The other things that helped me in this process were the experiential-based retreats[153] of Pathways and The Road Adventure.

Thought question(s): what has your spiritual growth been like to date? How would you like it to change?

---

[152] smile.amazon.com/Search-Significance-Seeing-Worth-Through-ebook/dp/B006X50SLM
[153] see: Chapter Nineteen: Experiential-Based Retreats, page 71

Chapter Twenty-Two: Groups

If you want to go fast, go alone.
If you want to go far, go with others.
~~ African Proverb

Some of the tools described previously in the book are inherently done with others. The experiential-based retreats[154] is one that requires other people in the process. However, many of the tools are typically done by yourself (journaling, for example), or with one other person like a coach (many or most of the assessments).

However, it's interesting that almost anything can be enhanced by bringing more people into the activity. Certainly many if not most of the assessments can be done with a group of people instead of individually, and this is good news for businesses as the cost for a team is likely quite a bit less than the cost if all the individuals went through it separately.

Many books can be enhanced though a group Book Study, where a group goes through a section of the book between every meeting. Meetings are often weekly, and you cover one or a few chapters. The accountability of being part of the group, plus the shared insights as people discuss the book, can greatly enhance the experience.

Bible studies, in churches or life groups or even online, provide the same experiences for the Bible.

Many college students prefer studying in a shared space like a library. Even if they study alone at the library, there is some sense of accountability and many students report greater focus and success.

And look at how many people go to coffee shops like Starbucks in order to work among other people. Even the "open office" concept has evolved to provide options for work or study in a shared space.

Mastermind groups[155] are great resources for their members, because the group is organized around some aspect of compatibility (age, profession, business, purpose, hobby, interest, etc.). The group then

---

[154] see: Chapter Nineteen: Experiential-Based Retreats, page 71
[155] wikipedia.org/wiki/Mastermind_group

meets, in person or virtual, and tackles problems presented by people in the group. The idea is that the power of the group "mastermind" is greater than the power if you sum up all the individuals. This is because good things happen when people are together. I am a member of a peer mastermind group of Professional Christian Coaches. Just today (as I write this), I was helped with some thoughts on my future branding and marketing through this group.

And don't rule out the power of even a group of two for what you might think of as a solitary activity. As I write this, I am home alone writing this chapter on my desktop computer. However, I have group accountability, because I am using a Focusmate[156] session which allows me to connect with Tim, a student somewhere else in the world who is studying for a Calculus exam tomorrow. We have video feeds so we can glance at each other. Knowing someone, even a stranger, could be watching really helps me concentrate on what I'm working on, and ignore distractions. As a matter of fact, large sections of this book were completed during Focusmate sessions.

While there are certainly benefits to groups, there are also drawbacks. A group is tougher to coordinate in terms of time and space. Groups that continue to meet for a long time typically need a leader or two that keeps the group moving and motivated, and if the leader loses interest, the group disperses unless a new leader rises to the occasion.

Thought question(s): what are the groups where you have participated, and what were the results?

---

[156] focusmate.com/dashboard

Section Four:

RECOMMENDATIONS

This section contains an evaluation process that could point you to the tools that would be most useful to you at the moment.

> Uncommunicated expectations are nothing
> more than premeditated resentments.
> ~~ Dale Young's take on a saying
> he heard in Pathways.

Evaluation

Hopefully I have provided quite a few new things and references for you to consider along your journey to significance. Which of these should you pursue now?

Part of that answer has to be questions back to you:
- Why do you want to go on or continue on this journey?
- What is the driving force?
- How quickly do you have to move?
- Where are you starting?
- Who is available to help you?

I know, that's not a lot of help — but then this is a (ICF-style) coaching book, not a consultant/expert book. However, here are some general rules:
- First of all, pray! Ask God to help you figure it out — He will!
- If all of this is new to you, and there is not a lot of urgency, start with the least investment of time and money, and build from there.
- If you already have some of the basic tools (i.e. low time and cost investment) and they fit you well, and you need more, then move up the scale.
- If something on this map (in this book) sounds exciting and useful to you, consider that higher on your priority list.
- If you're totally lost as to your next steps, then talk with someone in your Core or Close circles[157] and get their thoughts.
- Consider talking with a mentor or coach.

With any growth plan, you have both a time investment and a monetary investment. In addition, there are phases to consider. For example, let's say that you've decided that you want to take a particular assessment. If so, do you know somebody who can administer that assessment? If you don't, there is likely additional time (and potentially expense) to find someone that can administer it. And

---

[157] see: Relationship Bullseye, page 23

once you have the results, what do you do with them? That could be additional time and expense.

Let's do a general breakdown of "low to high time investment" and "low to high cost investment". Note the cutoffs of four hours of time and $250 of cost are arbitrary and are there to provide a general idea for you to do more research. In addition, there might be deals that lower the cost or provide a subset of the item which lowers the time, potentially putting the item in a different category.

Items with low time investment (less than four hours) and low cost investment (less than $250):
- Most assessments
- Chapter Fourteen: Writing / Journaling / Diaries
- Chapter Fifteen: Affirmations
- Chapter Seventeen: Books
- Music
- Chapter Eighteen: Podcasts
- Some Chapter Twenty-One: Spiritual Growth

Items with low time investment (less than four hours) and high cost investment (greater than $250):
- Some assessments
- Some Chapter Twenty-One: Spiritual Growth

Items with high time investment (greater than four hours) and low cost investment (less than $250):
- Peer Mastermind Chapter Twenty-Two: Groups
- Walk to Emmaus
- Possibly some assessments
- Some Chapter Twenty-One: Spiritual Growth

Items with high time investment (greater than four hours) and high cost investment (greater than $250):
- The WeAlign Strengths Alignment Process (SAP)
- Pathways and The Road Adventure
- Chapter Twenty: Coaching
- Some Chapter Twenty-One: Spiritual Growth
- Most Chapter Twenty-Two: Groups

Hopefully this list will provide you at least a starting point for more in-depth exploration.

If you are still confused, then reach out to me. I reserve a portion of my time each week and month to help people figure this out. Go to the contact page on my website[158] and submit a request to discuss your growth.

Thought question: what is your next step?

---

[158] coachdale.com/contact

> Finishing is better than starting.
> Patience is better than pride.
> ~~ Ecclesiastes 7:8, NLT

This is the final chapter in the book! Congratulations on making it here!

I would love your feedback!

What worked for you? What didn't?

How can I improve this book in the future?

How has this book proven valuable to you?

To provide feedback, go to the page[159] on my website where all the links are in live, clickable electronic form. There's a feedback form on that site where you can submit your thoughts.

---

[159] bit.ly/lsk_id